Sunset

faux and decorative painting

BY CHRISTINE E. BARNES AND THE EDITORS OF SUNSET BOOKS

MENLO PARK, CALIFORNIA

SUNSET BOOKS

VICE PRESIDENT AND GENERAL MANAGER: Richard A. Smeby
VICE PRESIDENT AND EDITORIAL DIRECTOR: Bob Doyle
PRODUCTION DIRECTOR: Lory Day
OPERATIONS DIRECTOR: Rosann Sutherland
RETAIL SALES DEVELOPMENT MANAGER: Linda Barker
EXECUTIVE EDITOR: Bridget Biscotti Bradley
ART DIRECTOR: Vasken Guiragossian
SPECIAL SALES: Brad Moses

STAFF FOR THIS BOOK

SENIOR EDITOR: Linda J. Selden
COPY EDITOR: Carol Boker
ART DIRECTOR/PAGE LAYOUT: Alice Rogers
DECORATIVE PAINTER: Shauna Oeberst Gallagher
PHOTOGRAPHER: Jayson Carpenter
PHOTO STYLIST: Cynthia Del Fava
CONTRIBUTING EDITOR: Mara Wildfeuer
PHOTO COORDINATOR: Carrie Dodson
PRODUCTION ASSISTANCE: Linda Bouchard
PREPRESS COORDINATOR: Eligio Hernandez
PROOFREADER: Mary Roybal
INDEXER: Phyllis Elving

10 9 8 7 6 5 4 3 2 1

First printing June 2004. Copyright © 2004,
Sunset Publishing Corporation, Menlo Park, CA 94025.
First edition. All rights reserved, including the right of
reproduction in whole or in part in any form.

ISBN 0-376-01410-5
Library of Congress Control Number: 2003115473
Printed in Hong Kong.

For additional copies of *Faux and Decorative Painting*
or any other Sunset book, call 1-800-526-511 or visit us
at *www.sunset.com*.

COVER: Deep-toned Parchment, page 44; *DECORATIVE PAINTER:*
Shauna Oeberst Gallagher; *COVER DESIGN:* Vasken Guiragossian;
PHOTOGRAPHER: Thomas J. Story; *PHOTO STYLISTS:* Cynthia Del
Fava, Laura Del Fava; Fixtures courtesy of *Plumbing N' Things*
(650) 363-7333

DECORATIVE PAINT

CHRISTINE E. BARNES: 100, 118, 128, 136, 138, 140
THOM BRUCE VENETIAN PLASTER: 33
MELINDA D. DOUROS: 124, 130
HEIDI M. EMMETT: 60, 94, 96
RICHARD FORD: 26 left
SHAUNA OEBERST GALLAGHER/ARTISTIC DESIGNS, INC.:
24, 25, 26–27 center, 27 right, 28, 30, 31, 32, 36, 40,
44, 47, 50, 54, 57, 62, 66, 68, 71, 74, 78, 81, 84, 86,
88, 98, 103, 106, 109, 115, 121
WILLEM RACKÉ STUDIO, INC.: 22 bottom right
D. KIMBERLY SMITH: 21 left, 94, 130
DEBRA S. WEISS: 96, 112

INTERIOR DESIGN

JODY ALLEN/JA DESIGNS: 47, 57
NANCY ESLICK INTERIOR DESIGN: 28–29 center
JENNIFER HOLLOWAY/DESIGN GALLERIA BY
    VALENTINE, INC.: 27 right, 40, 106, 121
RFdc: 33
JEANESE ROWELL DESIGN, INC.: 26 left
MICHELE SIMMONS/DESIGN GALLERIA BY
    VALENTINE, INC.: 62, 68, 88

PHOTOGRAPHY

ALL PHOTOS BY JAYSON CARPENTER EXCEPT AS
NOTED BELOW:
CHERYL FENTON: 26 left
JAMIE HADLEY: 22 bottom, 29 left, 33
STEVEN MAYS: 17
E. ANDREW MCKINNEY: 21 left, 94–97, 100–102, 112–114,
    124–125, 130–132

foreword

Paint has long possessed a well-earned reputation as the least expensive, fastest, and easiest way to redo a room. Simply put, you get a lot for your decorating dollars and time when you spend them on paint. By itself, paint is great.

But something special happens when you combine latex paint with glazing liquid, a milky substance that has the properties of paint, minus the color. What was opaque paint turns into a sheer curtain of color that can be spread thin for a translucent effect, or layered for a denser, more complex look. Needless to say, the creative possibilities in faux and decorative paint increase exponentially with glazes.

None of this is new, of course. Surfaces decorated with paint date back to Roman times and earlier. A resurgence of interest in the look of antiquity fuels the current popularity of new materials such as Venetian plaster and metallic paints, as well as existing materials like powder pigments, kraft paper, even joint compound.

Fresh takes on old favorites are just as much a part of the decorative paint scene. Stencils and stamps add bright color and bold design to surfaces; faux denim, taffeta, and rickrack give walls the illusion of fabric; loosely painted squares of colors become wall art.

No matter which of the 37 projects in this book you tackle first, allow yourself plenty of time to practice the technique and complete your walls. You'll love your new room, and the satisfaction and pleasure that naturally follow from hard work and success will be your reward.

contents

7 basics

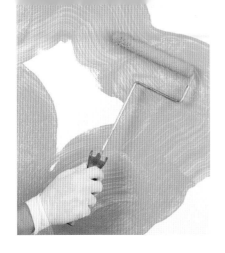

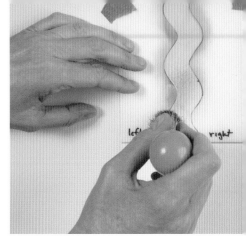

35 techniques

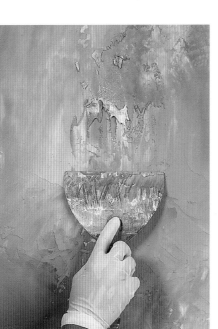

As you look through the examples of decorative paint in this book, you might wonder, "Can I really do this—and do it well?"

basics

You can. It's not necessary to be a professional painter to create beautiful walls in your home. What it does require is an eagerness to learn the fundamentals and a willingness to try new tools and techniques.

Paint, glaze, cheesecloth, and brushes—these are the essential ingredients in most of the projects you'll see on the following pages. Latex (water-based) paint and glazing liquid make cleanup a snap. Almost all of the tools are inexpensive and readily available at paint stores and home centers. Two recipes for glazes keep it simple and take the guesswork out of mixing

paint and glazing liquid in the proper proportions.

Step-by-step instructions for applying a base coat of paint and techniques for manipulating glaze on walls come next. Look through these sections now to get a feel for how it's done; then return to them when you're ready to begin your project.

Choosing colors is always a challenge, and the presence of glazing liquid adds an extra element to the process. A few strategies for determining your color preferences, plus color-and-glaze tips from the pros, will help you narrow your choices. You'll find extra inspiration in the mini-gallery of ideas at the end of this chapter.

But before you make plans to decorate your home with paint and glaze, spend some time in this chapter. Every successful project begins here, with the basics.

tools and materials

The following tools and materials are grouped by purpose: basic painting supplies, measuring and marking tools, and decorative painting supplies.

BASIC PAINTING SUPPLIES

You'll find these supplies at paint stores, hardware stores, and home centers. Buy the best tools and supplies you can afford for your project; quality tools ensure good results.

standard roller frame and roller cover Choose a roller with a steel frame, an expandable wire cage (the portion that slips inside the roller cover), and a handle threaded with a metal sleeve to accommodate an extension pole. Nine-inch roller covers for standard rollers come in various naps: $\frac{1}{4}$ inch for smooth walls, $\frac{3}{8}$ inch for semi-smooth or lightly textured walls, and $\frac{1}{2}$ inch or higher for heavily textured walls.

paint tray A paint tray is the standard application container for applying a base coat of latex paint to walls. Use it with disposable liners, which you can discard or clean and reuse.

bucket and paint rack For large jobs, use a 5-gallon bucket fitted with a metal roller grid to hold primer and base-coat paint. Cover the bucket with a wet towel if you take a break from painting.

stir sticks and paint keys When you buy your paint, ask for plenty of stir sticks and at least one paint key; they are usually free.

synthetic brushes You'll need a synthetic-bristle brush to fill in with paint at the edges after rolling on the base coat. A $2\frac{1}{2}$-inch brush with a tapered end is ideal for this task.

painter's tape Several types of tape are available to painters. Blue painter's tape (for interiors) comes in various widths; 1- or 2-inch tape works well for protecting trim and taping off stripes. Brown paper painter's tape has one sticky edge; it provides wider protection for adjacent surfaces. Never use standard masking tape—it is likely to lift paint from the surface you are trying to protect. However, to create a pattern of narrow lines on a surface (see Venetian Plaster Diamonds, page 74), you will need $\frac{1}{4}$-inch-wide masking tape, available at paint stores or auto paint shops.

gloves Always wear gloves to protect your skin from chemicals. Inexpensive disposable latex gloves allow flexible movement but wear out quickly; they're sold in bags or boxes. Heavy-duty rubber gloves are fine for cleanup and for techniques that don't require delicate handwork.

drop cloths Canvas drop cloths with rubber backing are the safest and most effective. Plastic is very slippery, and canvas alone won't protect against spilled paint. Invest in a good drop cloth and wash it as needed.

curved painter's tool This versatile tool has a crescent blade for scraping excess paint off a standard roller. It's also handy for opening paint cans.

2-inch painter's tape

1-inch painter's tape

$\frac{1}{4}$-inch masking tape

Paper tape

putty knife After masking a surface with blue painter's tape or brown paper tape, burnish along the tape edges with this tool.

bucket Keep a 5-gallon bucket filled with fresh water ready to clean your tools and rags as you go.

clean towels and rags You'll need towels and rags for myriad tasks. Paint stores sell clean rags by the box. Heavy paper rags on a roll, much like paper towels, are an easy alternative. Old cotton T-shirts work, too.

stepladder or step stool A sturdy stepladder or step stool is necessary for reaching high places when applying the base coat and doing decorative techniques.

MEASURING AND MARKING TOOLS

Decorative paint techniques that involve marking straight lines or sections of walls require various measuring and marking tools.

steel tape measure This rigid tape measure is the most accurate tool for marking large increments on a wall, such as the spacing for diamonds (page 74). Have a helper hold the end of the tape while you measure and mark the wall.

metal straightedge A 3- or 6-foot metal straightedge makes it easy to draw long, straight lines on walls.

carpenter's level You'll need a carpenter's level to mark accurate horizontal and vertical lines. Choose one with rubber "feet" on one side to avoid marring the wall.

rotary cutting tools Acrylic rotary rulers, available at fabric stores and quilt shops, are helpful for measuring and marking stripes. To cut stencils, use a rotary cutting mat.

plumb bob Attach this weighted guide to the ceiling, close to the wall, to help you drag straight lines.

pencils and chalk A standard #2 pencil, a colored pencil, and blackboard chalk are the only marking tools you'll need.

DECORATIVE PAINTING TOOLS

A few simple, inexpensive, and widely available painting tools work for most of the techniques presented in this book. Several techniques require more specialized tools, but even these are commonly stocked by full-service paint stores and home centers.

mini-roller frame and roller cover A 6-inch roller frame with matching roller cover is the best tool for applying glaze. Lightweight and easy to maneuver, this small roller deposits just the right amount of glaze on the surface. For most techniques, use a low-nap roller cover.

trim roller and roller cover A 3- or 4-inch roller with matching roller cover makes easy work of applying glaze or paint to small areas, such as narrow stripes.

unbleached cheesecloth For manipulating glaze across the wall, you'll use a pom-pom (page 18) made of cheesecloth. Buy unbleached cheesecloth found in the tile department, not the paint section, of home centers. Cheesecloth sold for use with tile is virtually lint-free and holds up to repeated use. Wash and dry the cheesecloth to remove the sizing.

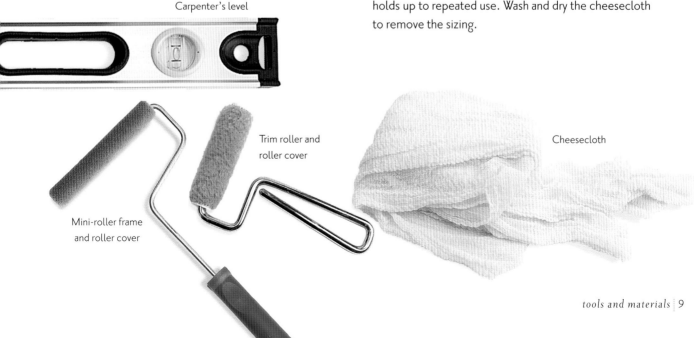

Carpenter's level

Trim roller and roller cover

Cheesecloth

Mini-roller frame and roller cover

chip brushes Use inexpensive, natural-bristle chip brushes to apply, stipple, and drag glazes. They tend to shed, so fan and tug at the end of the brush to dislodge loose bristles before you use it. Chip brushes are considered disposable, but they can be washed and reused.

commercial stippler Made of hog-hair or horsehair bristles imbedded in a large ferule (the base of the brush), a commercial stippler is designed to be pounced or tapped, rather than brushed, over the surface. Used specifically to stipple, it is an expensive but worthwhile tool if you are working over a large area.

badger blender brush If you can afford only one decorative paintbrush, buy a badger blender. This softening brush blends and refines the glaze after it has been stippled, giving the finish a truly professional look. Glaze dries quickly on the tips of the bristles, so have a damp rag handy to clean the end of the brush immediately after each use.

6-inch synthetic brush You'll need this wide, thick brush to apply generous amounts of paint for Color Blending (page 138).

stencil brushes These blunt, cylindrical brushes made of hog hair are used to pounce and swirl paint or stencil cream onto the wall through a stencil. Buy the highest quality brushes you can afford for the most even application.

artist's brushes A few projects call for detail work, such as narrow lines or highlights. The materials list will specify a #8 round or filbert brush.

containers for mixing glazes A 2½-quart bucket with a lid is ideal for mixing and storing glazes. Plastic containers with lids designed for food work well for small batches of glaze. (Never reuse any containers for food.)

sea sponge Use a natural sea sponge to apply powder pigment washes (page 79) over Venetian plaster or a base coat of latex paint. Choose a rounded (not jagged) sponge with medium pores.

cellulose sponge A common kitchen sponge is used to rub and blend powder pigments; buy a sponge with small or medium pores.

venetian plaster This smooth, thick material is applied with steel spatulas (page 72) and burnished to a high-gloss, marblelike surface.

Chip brushes

Commercial stippler

Sea sponge

Badger blender brush

Wide synthetic brush

Artist's brush #8

Stencil brushes

steel spatulas Use blue steel "spats" to apply Venetian plaster; the materials list with each project specifies the sizes. You'll need to sand one side of each spat's blade with fine (200-grit) sandpaper to sharpen; hold the spat with the sharpened side against the wall when applying the plaster.

plaster trough A plaster trough holds small batches of Venetian plaster transferred from the can; replace the lid on the can to keep the plaster moist. You'll also need a trough for projects that use wallboard joint compound.

wallboard joint compound All-purpose joint compound is available by the box or bucket. For projects that use just a little compound, such as Bas Relief (page 109), a 12-pound container should suffice. For techniques that cover the entire wall with joint compound, such as Textured Imprints (page 106) and Terra Fresco (page 98), experiment on a 4-foot sample board (page 19) to estimate the amount needed.

taping knife Use a 6-inch stainless-steel taping knife to drag and spread joint compound.

kraft paper This heavy brown paper required for Papier Collé (page 103) is available at art stores and framing shops.

wallpaper paste Adhere kraft paper to the wall with a coating of heavy-duty wallpaper paste.

wood-graining tool Typically used to simulate the look of wood, this "rocker" also creates the illusion of taffeta (page 115).

pastry bag with tip You'll use a standard pastry bag filled with joint compound and fitted with a ¼-inch tip to make raised designs for Bas Relief (page 109).

rubber stamps and stamp pads Stores devoted to stamping and paper crafts have the largest supply of rubber stamps. Choose stamp pads with indelible ink.

repositionable spray adhesive Removing and repositioning a stencil is easy with this spray adhesive. Read the label recommendations carefully for best results.

concentrated liquid acrylic paints Artist's liquid acrylic paint in small plastic jars has the ideal consistency and color concentration for stenciling. Myriad colors are available, from brilliant to muted.

stencil creams These solid, oil-based creams come in small pots and impart soft, misty color to walls.

Pastry bag

Rubber stamps

Steel spats

Taping knife

Taffeta rocker

Concentrated liquid acrylics

Stencil creams

about primer and paint

To provide the appropriate surface for glaze, walls must be prepared with primer and base-coat paint to create what is known as a "body of paint."

primer Your walls may or may not require priming before you begin a decorative paint technique. Here's what to do under various circumstances:

- On new walls that have never been primed, apply a coat of latex-based PVA (polyvinyl acetate) sealer to the sheetrock before applying a base coat to the walls.

- In new production or custom homes where the walls are freshly painted, you can skip the priming step and proceed to applying the base coat to the walls.

- To use your existing paint color as the base coat (only if your walls are clean), apply a coat of clear glazing liquid (page 16) before beginning a decorative technique.

- If your existing paint is more than five years old, you should prime the walls. If it's less than five years old, you can apply the base coat over it.

take note

WHAT IS A GLAZE?

It's important to understand the difference between "glazing liquid" (page 16) and "a glaze." Simply put, latex glazing liquid is the colorless medium that, when mixed with latex paint or universal tints (facing page), makes a glaze. Glazing liquid comes milky white (it dries clear) and is the same consistency as paint. In fact, it is sometimes referred to as "paint without the color."

latex paint Latex (water-based) paint is practical for faux and decorative paint finishes for several reasons: It dries quickly (usually in little more than an hour), is nearly odorless, and cleans up easily with soap and water.

Latex paint alone is opaque; once it is mixed with latex glazing liquid, the resulting glaze is somewhat transparent. The degree of transparency depends on the ratio of paint to glazing liquid; the more glazing liquid, the more transparent the glaze (see "Mixing Glazes," page 16).

Glazing liquid lightens paint significantly. To compensate when choosing paint for a glaze, find the desired finished color on a paint strip; then buy the next darkest paint color on the same strip. When the walls are complete, you'll have the color you wanted.

Latex paint

Universal tint in bottle or tube

Choose the highest-quality latex paint you can afford for your project. Premium paint has the greatest quantity of acrylic resin, up to 100 percent, making it easier to apply and more durable over time.

sheen   Descriptive terms for paint sheens vary from brand to brand, but the most commonly used—from lowest to highest sheen—are flat, eggshell, pearl, satin, semigloss, and gloss. There is no industry standard for sheens, and they vary slightly from one manufacturer to another. Most paint companies offer paint strips that show the range of sheens for easy comparison.

Sheen matters when you choose a base-coat paint. Glaze slides around on a base coat of eggshell, pearl, or satin paint, making it easy for you to work with the mixture on the surface. Over a base coat of flat paint, glaze is absorbed and becomes splotchy when dry.

Most of the techniques in this book call for a base coat of satin paint; eggshell or pearl finish will work as well. To mix a glaze using latex paint, choose paint of the same sheen as your base coat.

universal tints   These pure, concentrated pigments are used to color all custom-mixed paint you buy at the paint store. When mixed with glazing liquid, universal tints create a veil of sheer color. Available in bottles or tubes—bottled tints are more concentrated—universal tints contain no binders and are not permanent until combined with glazing liquid.

powder pigments   Mixed with water, powder pigments create transparent washes of color. Like universal tints, they contain no binders. To preserve the color, apply a top coat of clear acrylic sealer (page 17) once the walls are dry.

Powder pigments

painting how-tos

Although painting itself requires no special skills, a knowledge of general procedures and a few professional tricks and techniques will make the job easier and will result in a pleasing outcome.

painting sequence   The best way to prevent spattering paint on newly painted surfaces or touching a just-painted area is to follow a painting sequence. Plan to prime and paint the ceiling; then prime and paint the walls.

prep work   A successful paint treatment begins with careful preparation.

- Wipe the walls with clean rags to remove dust and tiny particles. If necessary, wash the walls with a solution of trisodium phosphate and water to remove grease or dirt.

- Gather the tools and materials needed to apply the base coat and the glaze (or other decorative finish); see "Tools and Materials," page 8.

- Lay canvas drop cloths to protect the floor.

- To mask baseboards or other trim, carefully apply 1- or 2-inch-wide blue painter's tape or brown paper tape.

How you mask the ceiling depends on how you plan to paint it:

- If you decide to paint the ceiling a different color, mask the walls at the ceiling line; then paint the ceiling. Once dry, remove the tape and mask the ceiling around its edges in preparation for painting the walls.

- If you want the ceiling the same color as the walls, it's not necessary to mask it.

- With crown molding, simply mask on either side of it.

applying the base coat Conventional wisdom dictates that you cut in with a brush and your base-coat paint before rolling the ceiling and walls, as shown below. You can do it the other way around, if you prefer, rolling on the base coat as close to the edges as possible, and then coming back with a brush to fill in any gaps. This approach can be faster because the remaining gaps tend to be narrower than the area covered with a brush if you cut in first.

The overall process for rolling on paint is the same whether you're painting a ceiling or a wall. To achieve a seamless look, roll the paint onto a fairly small area in a zigzag pattern, and then, without lifting the roller, roll over the same area in different directions to spread the paint. If you're painting a ceiling or a high wall, fit an extension handle onto your roller handle.

tip THE INSIDE EDGE OF A ROLLER COVER CAN ACCUMULATE PAINT, LEAVING A "BEAD" OF EXCESS PAINT WHEN YOU APPLY THE BASE COAT. IF YOU ARE PAINTING FROM LEFT TO RIGHT, HOLD THE ROLLER FRAME WITH THE METAL "STEM" TO THE RIGHT; THAT WAY, YOU'LL COVER ANY EXCESS PAINT AS YOU WORK ACROSS THE WALL. (TO WORK FROM RIGHT TO LEFT, HOLD THE FRAME WITH THE STEM TO THE LEFT.)

1 Load your roller with paint and discharge the excess on the bumpy or ridged surface of the paint tray. Starting near the ceiling, roll on the paint in a large zigzag pattern to cover an area approximately 3 by 4 feet. Roll diagonally upward first and keep the roller against the surface as you change direction. Maintain light, even pressure on the roller.

2 Without reloading or lifting the roller, roll back diagonally across the first zigzag pattern to fill in unpainted areas.

3 Again without reloading or lifting the roller, roll back over the same area, applying more pressure to the roller and keeping it nearly parallel to the 4-foot edge (the vertical edge shown here).

tip TO MINIMIZE SPATTERING, DISCHARGE EXCESS PAINT FROM YOUR ROLLER EVERY TIME YOU LOAD IT.

4 Repeat below the first section to complete the wall from ceiling to baseboard. Start the next section, near the ceiling, adjacent to the completed section.

5 When painting a ceiling, roll across the shorter dimension to minimize the drying time between passes.

1   2

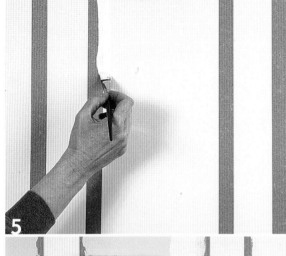

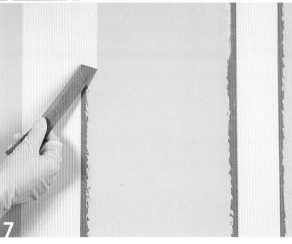

a tape trick Four of the projects in the following chapter require taping off the wall in preparation for painting stripes. Nothing is more frustrating than measuring, marking, and taping a wall for stripes, only to have paint seep under the tape and ruin the crisp effect. Professionals use the following trick to prevent seepage.

1 Apply the base coat to your walls (yellow in the example shown here); allow to dry. Apply a second coat; allow to dry.

tip FOR BEST COVERAGE, ALWAYS USE THE LIGHTER OF YOUR TWO CHOSEN COLORS FOR THE BASE COAT AND PAINT THE STRIPES THE DARKER COLOR.

2 With the carpenter's level and acrylic ruler held horizontally, measure and mark the stripe widths across the wall.

3 With the level and long straightedge held vertically at the marks made in the previous step, draw lines from the ceiling to the floor.

4 Tape off the stripes to be painted on the drawn lines. Remember that the edge of the tape goes on the line, with the tape itself in the area that will *not* be painted.

5 Before you paint the stripes the desired color (blue in this example), paint the edges of the tape with the base-coat color (yellow); allow to dry. This step seals the edge of the tape, and if any paint seeps under the tape, it will be the same color as the base coat. In other words, you are painting the edges of the tape with the color you wish to protect underneath—yellow, in this example.

6 Then roll on the stripe paint (blue), rolling just over the painted edges of the tape; allow to dry. Apply a second coat if needed; allow to dry.

7 Remove the tape gently at a 45-degree angle.

about glazes and top coats

It's not difficult to mix your own glazes using latex paint or universal tints. The process is more art than science, so be prepared to experiment a little with the ratio of paint (or universal tint) to glazing liquid until you achieve a color you like.

You can also buy ready-mixed colored glazes. They eliminate the step of mixing, but you won't find the color range possible by combining paint (or tints) with glazing liquid. When you need a dark antiquing glaze, such as for Porcelain Crackle (page 66), a commercial glaze is an easy option.

tip REMEMBER: WHEN YOU MIX GLAZING LIQUID WITH LATEX PAINT, THE RESULTING GLAZE IS SIGNIFICANTLY LIGHTER THAN THE ORIGINAL PAINT COLOR. WHEN CHOOSING PAINT TO MAKE A GLAZE, FIND THE DESIRED FINISHED COLOR ON THE PAINT STRIP, AND THEN BUY THE NEXT DARKER COLOR ON THE SAME STRIP.

mixing glazes There are two basic paint-and-glaze recipes used in the majority of techniques in this book. (A few techniques require slightly different recipes, and they are spelled out in the project directions.)

latex paint recipe 1

    1 part latex paint
    2 parts latex glazing liquid

This recipe yields a slightly more opaque glaze mixture that's appropriate for one-layer finishes, such as Deep-toned Parchment (page 44) and Strié (page 84). It has a shorter "open time" (the time the mixture stays wet and workable) than the next recipe, so you must work quickly.

latex paint recipe 2

    1 part latex paint
    3 parts latex glazing liquid

This recipe yields a slightly more transparent glaze mixture that's ideal for light or layered finishes, such as Bas Relief (page 109) and Aged Bronze (page 62). Use this recipe when you want more of the base-coat color showing through the glaze.

If you wish to experiment with the ratio of paint to glazing liquid, remember that the greater the ratio of paint to glazing liquid, the more opaque the finish will be. With any glaze recipe, gradually add the paint to the glazing liquid (not the other way around) until you achieve a color slightly darker than the desired finished color.

tip IF THE GLAZING MEDIUM YOU PURCHASE IS THICK, LIKE PUDDING, ADD A LITTLE WATER TO MAKE IT THE CONSISTENCY OF HEAVY CREAM. ALSO ADD A LITTLE WATER TO THE MIXTURE IF YOUR WALLS ARE HEAVILY TEXTURED.

universal tint recipe
Mixing glazes using universal tints is a very different process than mixing glazes with paint. Because universal tints are so concentrated, a little goes a very long way. When making a glaze with universal tints, add the pigment a drop or two at a time. Then mix the glaze thoroughly and test your chosen technique on a sample board (page 19) to determine if you need more tint.

estimating paint and glazing liquid To determine how much paint to buy for the base coat, you'll need to calculate the square footage of your walls. Measure the width of each wall, add up the widths, and then multiply by the wall height. Subtract the square footage of areas that won't be painted, such as windows and

Top coat

Glaze

doors. For the ceiling, multiply the width by the length. Ask your paint store to recommend the number of gallons needed to apply two coats to your walls and ceiling. In general, you can cover 300–400 square feet per gallon of paint.

To determine how much paint you will need to prepare a glaze, first calculate the total number of gallons of glaze required for your walls. In general, you can cover twice the square footage with glaze as you can with paint, or approximately 600–800 square feet per gallon of glaze.

Then turn to your chosen technique's recipe to determine how much paint and glazing liquid you need to make up each gallon of glaze. For example, if your recipe calls for I part paint to 3 parts glazing liquid, you will need I quart of paint and 3 quarts of glazing liquid to make up I gallon (4 quarts) of glaze mixture.

tip One quart of latex paint is almost always enough to mix a glaze for a small or average-size room.

For the beginner, it's easiest to mix up the glaze using quarts as your unit of measure. For example, if a recipe calls for I part paint to 2 parts glazing liquid, and you use quarts as your unit of measure, you'll get 3 quarts (or ¾ gallon) of glaze mixture. If your room requires a total of I½ gallons of glaze, you will need to double the quantity of paint and glazing liquid to maintain the correct proportions. Always mix up enough glaze for the entire project, plus a little extra, before you begin.

keeping glazes wet Latex glazes can dry quickly. To extend the open time of the glaze, work on a cool, damp day, preferably early in the morning. Heat, aridity, and strong afternoon sun dramatically speed the drying process. Also turn off air conditioning (or central heat) and overhead fans. If you must work on a warm day, lightly mist the wall with water in a spray bottle before you work each area.

top coats A few of the techniques in this book require a top coat to seal the surface. Look for latex clear acrylic sealer in the section of the store where glazing liquid is sold. Acrylic sealer comes in several sheens, typically matte, satin, and gloss.

For those projects requiring a sealer, matte or satin finish is appropriate. Refer to the can to determine how many gallons you'll need to cover your walls.

glazing how-tos

The steps with each project tell you which tool and technique to use to apply and work the glaze. Following are directions for the most-used tools and techniques:

masking adjacent surfaces Mask the ceiling and trim as you did before applying the base coat. If you'll be doing your chosen decorative finish on just one wall (or one wall at a time), also mask the adjacent walls at the corners with brown paper tape as follows:

1 Apply the paper tape with the sticky edge butted into the corner. To ensure a tight seal, run your fingers or a putty knife along the tape.

2 To remove the tape, peel one end and gently pull at a 45-degree angle. (If you pull the tape straight up, you're more likely to lift some of the paint.) If you have difficulty removing the tape, try loosening it with a hair dryer set on warm.

applying glaze with a mini-roller For most of the techniques in this book, you will apply the glaze using a 6-inch mini-roller fitted with a low-nap cover. Unless directed otherwise, roll on the glaze in a random, natural pattern over an area approximately 2 by 2 feet (see Antique Glazing, page 36). Applying glaze in this manner minimizes the number of wet edges; the fewer the edges, the less likely it is that demarcation lines will form. See the photo below for the correct and incorrect way to apply the glaze.

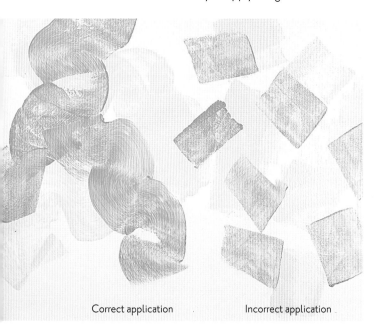

Correct application   Incorrect application

For some techniques, such as Strié (page 84) and Taffeta (page 115), you'll need to extend the just-rolled wet glaze to the ceiling line and the baseboard using a brush.

applying glaze with a chip brush When using a chip brush to apply glaze, as in Multicolor Faux (page 47), dunk the brush into the glaze and slap the sides of the brush against the inside of the container to keep the brush loaded, but not dripping, with paint. Do not run the brush against the container's edge—this action removes too much glaze.

forming a pom-pom Many of the projects call for a pom-pom made of cheesecloth (page 9) to blend and refine the glaze. The instructions will specify either a flat or a wrinkled pom-pom. A flat pom-pom yields a smoother finish, while a wrinkled pom-pom creates more pattern and visual texture. For either type, cut a length of laundered

cheesecloth equal to your "wingspan" (open arms). Pull apart the cloth widthwise to fluff it. Form the pom-pom as follows:

1 Drape the length of cheesecloth over your open hand (palm side up). Make sure the ends of the cheesecloth are approximately equal.

2 With your other hand, gather up both loose ends at once, folding them accordion-style toward your open hand.

3 Remove your open hand from under the cheesecloth and transfer the cloth to your other hand. Tuck under the loose edges or "tails" of cloth to form a smooth, rounded pom-pom.

4 To make a wrinkled pom-pom, allow folds of cloth to gather when you remove your open hand, creating a slightly wrinkled surface.

---

tip Have a bucket of fresh water and clean rags handy when you apply glaze. Rinse and re-form your pom-pom as soon as it becomes loaded with glaze; wipe away any glaze mistakes quickly with a clean, damp rag.

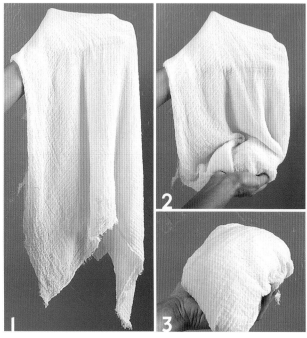

SAMPLE BOARDS

Decorative painting requires practice. Although it may seem like more work at the outset, experimenting on a sample board before you tackle your walls will save time and make the painting experience more enjoyable.

The least expensive material for sample boards is ⅛-inch standard hardboard, available at home centers and lumberyards. Hardboard comes in 4- by 8-foot sheets. For most projects, one sheet will be adequate. Have the sheet cut as follows:

- one piece, 4 by 4 feet
- four pieces, each 2 by 2 feet

Using a mini-roller, prime the pieces with latex primer; allow to dry. Apply a second coat of primer; allow to dry. Apply two coats of your base-coat paint, allowing the paint to dry between coats.

Practice your technique on the small pieces of hardboard to get a feel for the glaze and the tools. Then practice blending one section into another on the large piece of hardboard. When you're satisfied with the results, proceed to your walls.

blending with the blender brush Use just the tips of your blender brush to sweep across the surface lightly in a semicircular motion, blending the glaze. Do not hold the brush to the side or apply too much pressure; if you do, you'll create noticeable lines in the glaze. To minimize any lines, blend lightly in the opposite direction.

secrets of the pros Certain ways of working with glaze will help you achieve professional results:

- Whether you begin at the right or the left edge of a wall is up to you; the objective is to avoid smearing your work as you progress. In general, right-handed people are more comfortable working from left to right; left-handed people from right to left.

- For most decorative finishes, apply and manipulate the glaze on the upper, middle, and lower areas of one section of a wall. Then move to the side and repeat on the adjacent section of the wall.

- "Working wet," a term often used by faux finishers, means manipulating the glaze on the surface while it is still liquid and shiny, as in Deep-toned Parchment (page 44). Once the glaze begins to set up and dry, any attempt to pounce, stipple, or blend it will ruin the finish—a disaster referred to as a "burn" by the pros.

- You must maintain a wet edge when applying glaze in straight bands with the mini-roller, as in Plaid (page 88). This prevents demarcation lines from forming as the finish dries.

- Corners are easier to navigate than you might think. With many finishes, you simply "wrap," or continue, the treatment around corners, enabling you to work all the way around the room without stopping. If you plan to do just one wall in your chosen finish, mask off the adjacent walls at the corners to avoid getting paint where you don't want it (see "Masking Adjacent Surfaces," page 17).

WHAT'S EASY?

Surprisingly, one-glaze techniques, such as Antique Glazing (page 36), are more challenging than multiple-glaze techniques, such as Parchment (page 40) or Multicolor Faux (page 47). With just one glaze, you must feather the edges of the glaze evenly or demarcation lines will form where you stop and start the sections. With two or more glazes, any inconsistencies where sections meet seem to meld into the finish. If you're a rookie, opt for a two-glaze (or more) technique on your first project.

choosing colors

Color is the essence of every faux and decorative paint technique, yet choosing color is probably the most intimidating step in the process. All of the projects in this book specify the colors used, and many also include sample dots of the actual paints and glazes (see page 35). But what if you must choose different colors, ones that work with your existing furnishings? Perhaps you're starting over and plan to create a whole new palette. How do you go about it? Where do you begin? As obvious as it sounds, you should start with what you like.

DETERMINE YOUR COLOR PREFERENCES

Many of us never think about decorating with color until faced with hundreds of paint chips on display at the paint store or home center. That's when doubt sets in. You can prevent a panic attack and minimize your frustration if you ask yourself the following questions about color:

light or dark? Are you happiest in a room painted a light color, or do you like the intimacy of a room with dark walls? The lightness or darkness of color, a quality referred to as its "value" by designers, has as much to do with the impact of color as the color itself. In general, light colors recede, dissolving the boundaries of a room and making the space appear larger. Dark colors advance, defining the room and creating the illusion of a more intimate space. Once you decide on the effect you want to create—expansive or cozy—you can focus on colors in values that will achieve that look.

Light-value colors (above) make a room feel light and airy; dark-value colors (left) contract space.

tip Color looks more intense on walls than it does on a paint chip or a sample board. To get the desired look, select a more muted version of the color you think you want.

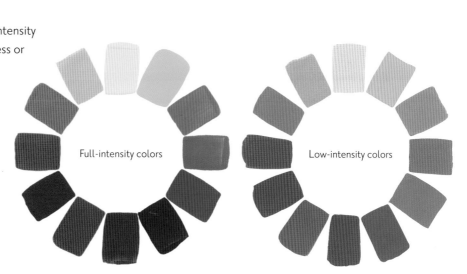

Cool blue (above left) is refreshing and calming; warm gold (above) is earthy and energetic.

warm or cool? All colors have a visual "temperature." Yellow, red, and orange are warm; they are considered lively and advancing because they seem closer to the viewer. That's why warm colors on walls make a room so inviting. Green, blue, and violet are cool; they are referred to as receding because they seem more distant. Cool color makes a room feel more open. In deciding whether you want warm or cool color on your walls, you automatically narrow the choices.

bright or muted? The intensity of color refers to its brightness or dullness, and more than any other color characteristic, intensity sets the mood in a room. The colors shown on the color ring at near right are full intensity; the colors shown on the color ring at far right are low intensity. Colors of similar

Full-intensity colors

Low-intensity colors

intensity—willow green, sandstone, and slate blue, for example—just seem to belong together. When choosing paint for several different glazes, select colors of the same or similar intensity.

what about neutrals? Many of the decorative finishes highlighted in this book feature neutral colors—and for good reason. Walls, by their sheer area, make a strong statement in a room. Neutral colors are livable and versatile over great expanses like walls.

Light neutrals, such as ivory, cream, and tan, play an important supporting role as base-coat colors for glazes. Darker versions, such as beige and camel, blend beautifully with glazing liquid and add subtle depth to walls when worked over lighter base coats. Low-intensity colors, such as khaki and olive drab, function as neutrals, too.

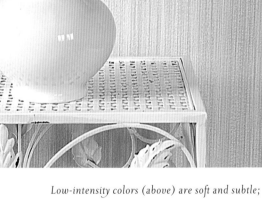

Low-intensity colors (above) are soft and subtle; intense colors (above right) are bright and lively.

Neutral colors, such as taupe (right), make a stunning backdrop for sophisticated furnishings.

LEARN FROM THE PROS

Let the experience of designers help you make good color choices:

- Paint as you see it in the can will dry both darker and stronger on your walls. Glaze, when manipulated over the surface of the wall, often looks lighter when dry. Think about these aspects when you're evaluating a base-coat color or a glaze.

- When choosing similar colors for a subdued finish, such as cream and tan used to create Parchment (page 40), make sure the values contrast enough to see a definite difference between the colors. If they are too close in value—both very light, for example—the wall will look like one color.

- When you choose your own colors for glazes, stick with related hues, such as medium terra cotta, dark terra cotta, and gold used to create Terra Fresco (page 98). If in doubt, select colors that are adjacent (rather than opposite) on the color ring. Opposite colors, known as complements, will appear to mix, creating an unattractive gray or brown cast to the walls.

DISCOVER THE MAGIC OF GLAZE

When mixed with glazing liquid, opaque paint becomes semitransparent, and the resulting glaze often appears luminous, as if light is coming from behind the surface. That's the fascination of faux and decorative techniques. As you choose colors for glazes, think about the interplay of light and color that occurs.

- Glazing liquid lightens paint at least one "step" on a paint strip. To get the look you like (and avoid disappointment), find the finished color you want on your paint strip, and then choose the next darker color on the same strip. That's the paint to buy for mixing your glaze.

- The color of your base-coat paint has a lot to do with the finished look of glazed walls. The same Antique Glazing mixture worked over a wall painted ivory (page 36) will look darker and heavier over a wall with a base coat of green (page 24). That's why it's so important to test not just your glaze, but your base-coat color, on a sample board (page 19).

take note

TEXTURE MATTERS

Texture always plays a role in decorating, but it takes center stage in faux and decorative paint. Unlike plain paint, glazes and other faux finishes contribute both actual texture—the feel of wrinkled paper in Papier Collé (page 103)—and visual texture—the illusion of supple leather in Chamois (page 60). Decorative techniques also lend subtle pattern to walls, such as the soft lines of vertical Strié (page 84).

Like color, the impact of texture depends on the size of the room. The larger the room, the greater the visual impact of textured walls. What appears to be an interesting blend of color and pattern on a 2- by 2-foot board may look busy and bold, even chaotic, on your walls if your room is large. To be sure, audition your chosen technique on a 4- by 4-foot board.

ABOVE: Powder-pigment washes sponged over a base coat of neutral-colored Venetian plaster create visual texture.

LEFT: Tissue paper, wrinkled slightly as it's pasted to the wall, contributes actual texture; glazes rubbed over the paper once it's dry enhance the textured surface. (See Sharpei, page 100.)

inspiring ideas

soft touches

Fanciful flowers made of joint compound (see Bas Relief, page 109) add real dimension to this nursery's walls. A lavender glaze over a pink base coat is soft and subtle; pink and green pearlescent paints accent the flowers and the stems.

The same sheer glaze (see Antique Glazing, page 36) appears semi-translucent over an off-white base coat (below) and opaque over a base coat of medium green (facing page).

specialty finishes

*The look of real wood,
known as "faux bois,"
results from brushing and
dragging darker glaze over
a lighter base coat.*

*Equal parts of gold metallic
latex paint and glazing liquid
comprise the glaze used in this
elegant version of Sharpei
(see page 100). The glaze was
rolled on the tissue-papered
walls, then pounced lightly
and rubbed in a back-and-
forth motion to work the
glaze into the creases.*

An Aged Bronze finish looks lighter when the glazes contain a higher ratio of glazing liquid to paint. (These glazes were 1 part paint to 3 parts glazing liquid; compare the effect to the finish on page 62.) Applying the glaze to just 50 percent of the surface area allows more of the off-white base coat to show through.

versatile stripes

Twelve-inch stripes in cream and soft blue provide a tailored backdrop for a mix of traditional colors and patterns.

FACING PAGE: It's not necessary to tape off these casual stripes before painting. Simply measure and lightly mark 15-inch-wide spaces on a base coat of lighter paint; then roll on darker paint as precisely as you can. Paint the squiggles freehand using a 1-inch-wide "bright" artist's brush; highlight with metallic paint.

Green and purple "rugby stripes" don't overpower a small laundry room because the colors are medium in value and low in intensity (see pages 20–22). To paint crisp stripes on textured walls, refer to "A Tape Trick," page 15.

multicolor effects

A Multicolor Faux finish (see page 47) created with four glazes—caramel, bark, camel, and dark chocolate— over a creamy golden base coat is both subtle and complex. Glazes consisting of 1 part paint to 2 parts glazing liquid (Recipe 1, page 16) are well suited to textured walls.

A multicolor technique looks dramatically different here, on smooth walls. Burnt sienna (a deep brick red) and dark burnt orange glazes are lightened by the same base coat used for the finish on the facing page.

Three warm glazes applied in varying proportions blend into one luminous finish. Deep red orange and dark burnt orange glazes contribute most of the color, approximately 40 percent each; a dark brown glaze adds the remaining 20 percent. The highly textured walls were first painted deep coral.

decorated ceilings

It requires a professional on scaffolding to paint a high-ceilinged entry, but you can achieve a similar look on a standard ceiling or walls. Begin with an ivory base coat, followed by layers of mauve, gold, and blue-green glazes, each in a ratio of 1 part paint to 3 parts glazing liquid. Before the glazes dry, use a clean pom-pom (page 18) to open up areas for clouds (see Cloudy Skies, page 54).

The Porcelain Crackle finish shown on page 66 continues to the coffered ceiling in this contemporary office. Large diamonds were measured, marked, and taped, and then glazed a golden bronze.

Venetian plaster is the backdrop for musical notes stenciled on the ceiling of this fantasy music room. A light touch with the stencil brush and opalescent white paint keep the effect ethereal.

A GED BRONZE, ANTIQUE GLAZING, PARCHMENT, STRIÉ—THE NAMES ALONE are enough to entice a beginner to pick up a brush.

If you are that beginner, or even if you've had a little experience with paint, you'll find all that you need to create a wealth of faux and decorative effects in this how-to chapter.

Each project contains a photo of the finished technique, a list of materials, and a brief introduction to the technique. Step-by-step instructions follow, with tips to guide you through the process and help you avoid the pitfalls. Accompanying those projects that require glazes, you'll also see fingertip dots of the actual glazes, such as the ones shown here.

Why the dots? Glazes made of paint and glazing liquid appear much darker on a mini-roller (or in a mixing container) than when they are spread over the wall with a cheesecloth pom-pom, chip brush, or other tool. Seeing the difference between the glaze and the way it looks on the wall will help you proceed with confidence.

There's more to decorative paint, however, than glazing techniques. Venetian Plaster has the look and feel of polished marble; Powder Pigments create transparent washes of color; Papier Collé offers a new twist on "wall paper"; Terra Fresco adds actual texture to walls. If you want to work with just paint, there are original techniques, including Color Blending, Floating Stencils, and Color Blocks.

Intrigued by the options? Choose a technique, gather the proper tools and materials, and begin painting.

techniques

antique glazing

This one-glaze technique veils a room in sheer color and delicate texture. The glaze is mixed using universal tints (see page 13) rather than latex paint, giving it a semi-transparent quality. ◆ *You'll work in sections, feathering the edges of the glaze for a seamless look. Once you apply the glaze, you must move quickly, so assemble your tools and other materials before you begin.*

materials

Basic painting supplies
   (page 8)

Standard roller frame
   with 9-inch roller cover

Mini-roller frame
   with 6-inch roller cover

Cheesecloth

Stippler brush*

Blender brush

Cream latex paint,
   satin finish, for base coat

Universal tints (page 13)
   in thalo green, yellow
   oxide, raw umber, and
   thalo blue for glaze

Latex glazing liquid

*As an alternative to a commercial
stippler (see page 10), tape two
3-inch chip brushes together with
masking tape.

1   Using the standard roller, apply a base coat of cream paint to the walls; allow to dry. Apply a second coat; allow to dry.

2   Mix the universal tints and glazing liquid to make the green glaze (see "Mixing Glazes," page 16).

3   Begin in the upper area of the wall, near a corner. Using the mini-roller, apply the glaze generously in a random, natural pattern that's approximately 2 by 2 feet. Leave some of the base coat showing in the center.

4   Using a flat cheesecloth pom-pom (page 18), pounce the edges. Rotate your wrist as you go to feather and blend the glaze. Keep the edges soft and irregular.

5   Move to the area where the glaze is still heavy and wet, and pounce outward, stopping short of the edge made in the previous step. Try to create subtle highs (areas of lighter color) and lows (areas of darker color) across the surface.

steps continue >

tip AVOID ROLLING ON THE GLAZE IN A SQUARE SHAPE; IF YOU DO, THE COMPLETED WALL WILL LOOK LIKE "PATCHWORK."

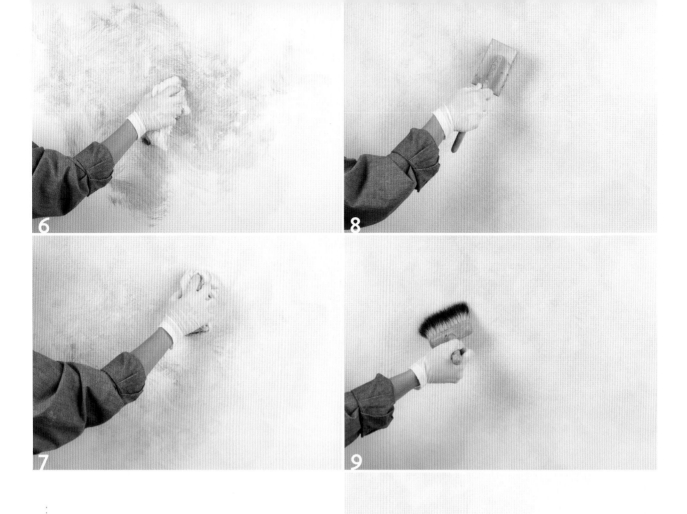

6   Rearrange your pom-pom to a clean area of the cheesecloth, and pounce the center area to refine the glaze.

7   Pounce outward to refine the glaze at the edges.

8   Use the stippler brush in a quick tapping motion to soften the glaze and eliminate tiny lines.

9   Using just the tips of the blender brush, sweep across the surface in a crisscross or semicircular motion to blend the glaze.

10 Stand back and look carefully at the section; blend the glaze more, if necessary.

tip DO NOT USE THE SIDE OF THE BLENDER BRUSH OR APPLY TOO MUCH PRESSURE; IF YOU DO, YOU'LL CREATE NOTICE-ABLE LINES. TO MINIMIZE ANY LINES, BLEND LIGHTLY IN THE OPPOSITE DIRECTION.

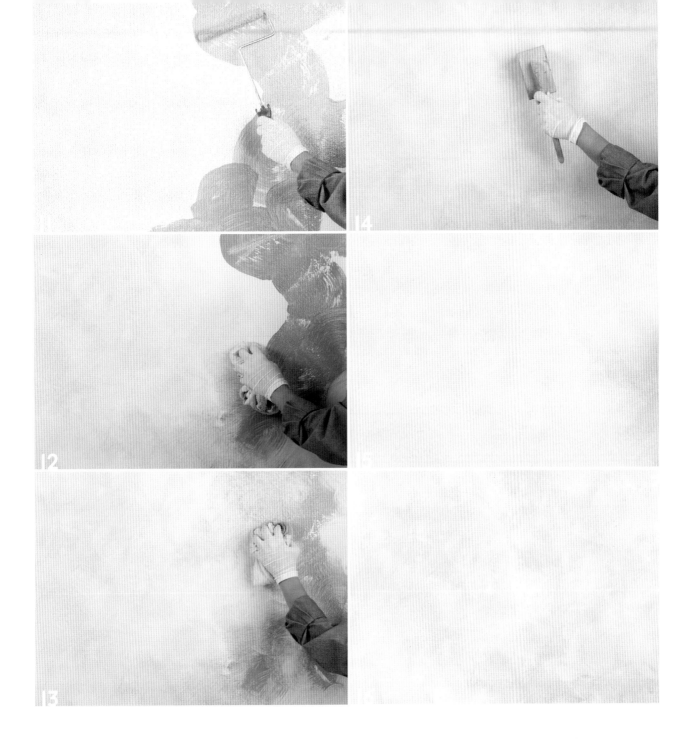

11 Apply the glaze to the adjacent area, making sure not to roll too close to the first section.

12 Pounce the edges to feather the color toward the first section.

13 Overlap the glaze only in the lightest area of the previously created edge. If you stray too far into the first section, the color will be darker where the edges overlap.

14 Use the stippler brush to soften the glaze.

15 Sweep the surface with the blender brush.

16 Continue working in the same manner, section by section, to complete the walls.

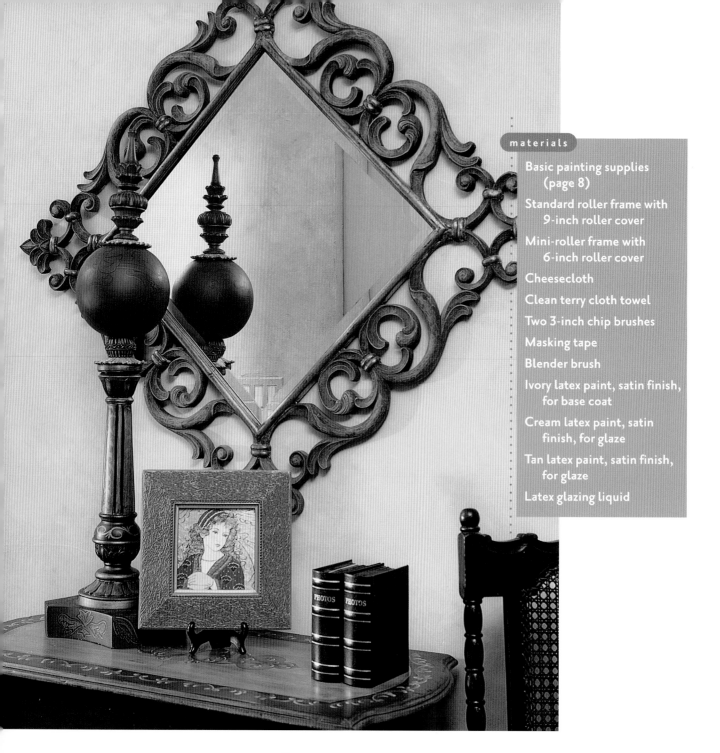

materials

Basic painting supplies
   (page 8)

Standard roller frame with
   9-inch roller cover

Mini-roller frame with
   6-inch roller cover

Cheesecloth

Clean terry cloth towel

Two 3-inch chip brushes

Masking tape

Blender brush

Ivory latex paint, satin finish,
   for base coat

Cream latex paint, satin
   finish, for glaze

Tan latex paint, satin finish,
   for glaze

Latex glazing liquid

parchment
This two-glaze faux finish is forgiving, making it an ideal technique for the novice. Because the glazes—each a mixture of latex paint and glazing liquid—are similar in color, imperfections in their application go unnoticed. ◆ To achieve a true parchment effect, apply the glaze generously and work wet (page 19), manipulating the glaze on the wall rather than lifting it off. Two chip brushes taped together for stippling make it easy to work in the corners and at the ceiling line.

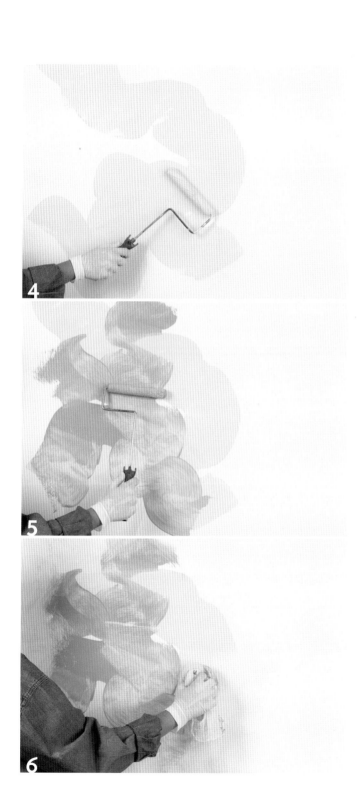

technique

1   Using the standard roller, apply a base coat of ivory paint to the walls; allow to dry. Apply a second coat; allow to dry.

2   Mix each glaze following this recipe: 1 part paint to 2 parts glazing liquid (see "Mixing Glazes," page 16).

3   Tape the chip brushes together with the masking tape; set aside.

4   Begin in the upper area of the wall, near a corner. Using the mini-roller, apply the cream glaze generously in a random, natural pattern that's approximately 2 by 2 feet. Leave plenty of the base-coat color showing.

5   Using the mini-roller, apply the tan glaze, rolling over some of the cream glaze and some of the base coat in a random, natural pattern. Don't roll in exactly the same pattern you used for the cream glaze.

6   Using a wrinkled cheesecloth pom-pom (page 18), pounce the outer edges and the areas where the two glazes meet. Rotate your wrist as you go to feather and blend the glazes. Keep the edges soft and irregular. Leave some areas of stronger color.

steps continue >

tip BE CAREFUL NOT TO REMOVE TOO MUCH GLAZE OR THE SURFACE WILL DRY AND YOU WON'T BE ABLE TO STIPPLE LATER.

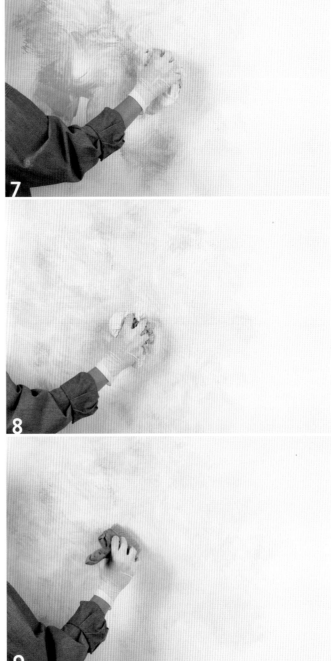

7   Move to the center area, where the glaze is still heavy and wet, and pounce outward, skipping over the surface and twisting your wrist as you go.

8   Rearrange your pom-pom to a clean area of the cheesecloth and continue pouncing to refine the glaze.

9   Holding the attached chip brushes perpendicular to the surface, stipple in a quick tapping motion to soften the glaze and eliminate tiny lines. Discharge accumulated paint on the tips of the brushes using the terry cloth towel. If your walls are textured, make sure you are working the glaze into the nooks and crannies.

10 Using just the tips of the blender brush, sweep across the surface in a crisscross or semicircular motion to blend the glaze (see Tip, page 38).

tip IF A VERTICAL LINE FORMS AS YOU STIPPLE, HOLD THE BRUSHES HORIZONTALLY AND STIPPLE OUT THE LINE. IF YOU HOLD THE BRUSHES VERTICALLY, YOU'LL JUST MAKE THE LINE BIGGER.

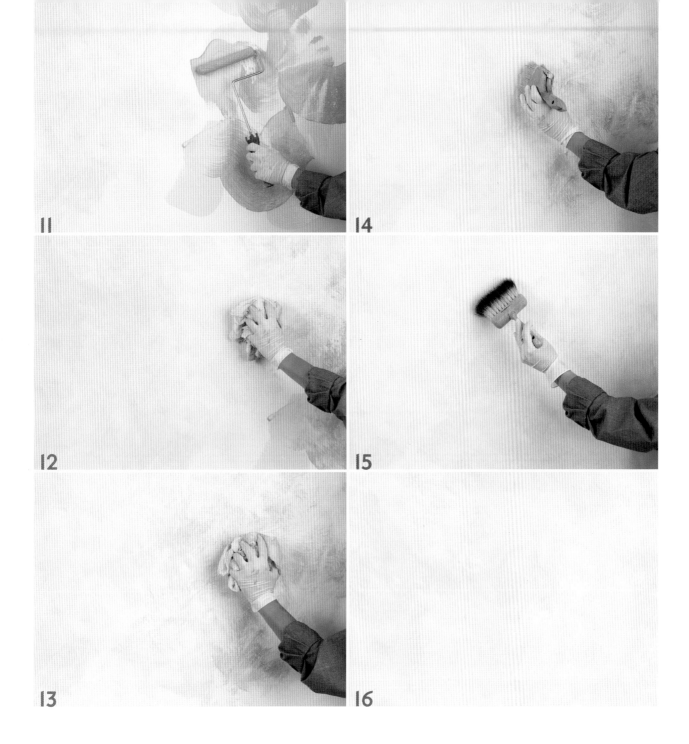

11 Using the mini-roller, apply the cream glaze, followed by the tan glaze, in the adjacent area. Make sure you do not roll too close to the just-completed section.

12 Pounce the edges to feather and blend the colors toward the first section.

13 Pounce in the center of the section, to refine the glaze where it is still heavy and wet.

14 Stipple the glaze as before.

15 Blend the glaze as before.

16 Continue working in the same manner, section by section, to complete the walls.

deep-toned parchment

With this dreamy faux finish, blending is everything. You manipulate the glaze using a cotton rag, rather than a cheesecloth pom-pom. A rag keeps the glaze heavy and wet on the surface, allowing you to blend and swirl the colors for a dramatic effect. ◆ Choose a medium-to-deep red that does not have blue undertones for the base coat and the glazes. You'll need yellow to make the lighter red glaze and black to make the darker red glaze. Experiment with mixing just the paint colors before you make the glazes.

1. Using the standard roller, apply a base coat of red paint to the walls; allow to dry. Apply a second coat; allow to dry.

2. To mix the paint for the glazes, add a small amount of yellow to the base-coat red to create the lighter color, and add a small amount of black to the base-coat red to create the darker color. Once you're satisfied with the colors, mix each glaze following this recipe: I part paint to 2 parts glazing liquid (see "Mixing Glazes," page 16).

3. Tape the chip brushes together with the masking tape; set aside.

4. Using the mini-roller, apply the lighter red glaze generously in a random, natural pattern.

5. Apply the darker red glaze, rolling over some of the lighter red glaze and the base-coat color.

6. Using a cotton rag, work the edges outward in a gliding motion. Twist your wrist as you go and skip over the surface to blend the colors and create subtle highs (areas of lighter color) and lows (areas of darker color). Return to the center, and work the areas where the two glazes meet to eliminate roller lines. The glaze should still be heavy and wet.

steps continue >

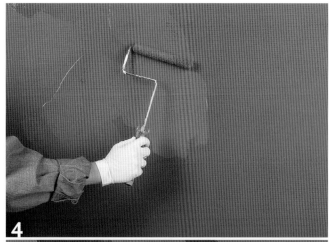

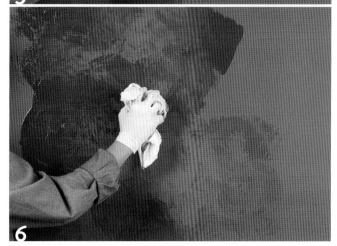

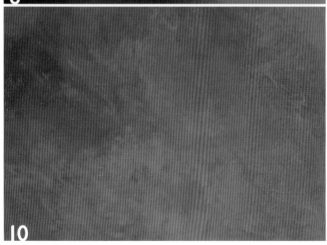

7 Holding the taped brushes perpendicular to the surface, stipple delicately in a quick tapping motion to blend the glazes. (Keep it light; if you're heavy-handed, you'll lose the highs and lows.)

tip To eliminate remaining roller lines, stipple them lightly with the corners of the brushes, twisting gently on contact.

8 Using just the tips of the blender brush, sweep across the surface in a crisscross or semicircular motion to blend the colors into a visual flow.

9 Move to the adjacent area and work the second section in the same manner, joining the edges seamlessly (see Steps 11–15, page 39).

10 Continue working, section by section, to complete the walls.

Basic painting supplies
(page 8)

materials

- Basic painting supplies (page 8)
- Standard roller frame with 9-inch roller cover
- Mini-roller frame with 6-inch roller cover
- Cheesecloth
- Three 4-inch chip brushes
- Masking tape
- One 3-inch chip brush
- One 2-inch chip brush
- Blender brush
- Cream latex paint, satin finish, for base coat
- Beige, light green, and medium green latex paint, satin finish, for glazes
- Latex glazing liquid

multicolor faux

One of the most versatile faux finishes, this multicolor technique uses three pale-to-medium colors in varying proportions over a light base coat. (This finish is just as successful with deep, dark colors.) ◆ *Different-size chip brushes make it easy to apply the glazes in distinctly different quantities; the example shown here is approximately 60 percent beige glaze, 30 percent light green glaze, and 10 percent medium green glaze. As with other two- or three-color finishes, imperfections in the application of the glazes tend not to show.*

1   Using the standard roller, apply a base coat of cream paint to the walls; allow to dry. Apply a second coat; allow to dry.

2   Mix each glaze following this recipe: 1 part paint to 2 parts glazing liquid (see "Mixing Glazes," page 16).

3   Tape two of the 4-inch chip brushes together with masking tape; set aside.

4   Dunk the remaining 4-inch chip brush into the beige glaze, and slap the sides against the inside of the container to keep the brush loaded, but not dripping, with paint. Apply the glaze generously in a random, natural pattern, using one side of the brush and then the other.

5   Using the 3-inch brush, apply a small quantity of the light green glaze over some of the beige glaze and the base-coat color.

6   Using the 2-inch brush, apply an even smaller quantity of the medium green glaze over the light green glaze.

7   Using a loose, flat cheesecloth pom-pom (page 18), pounce the edges. Rotate your wrist as you go to feather and blend the glazes.

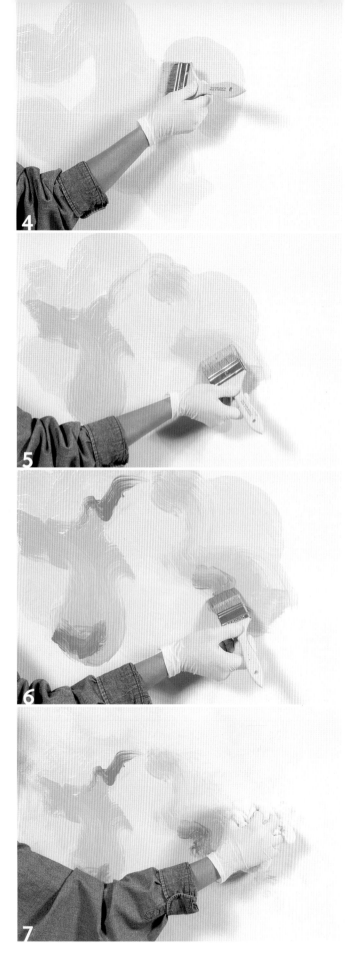

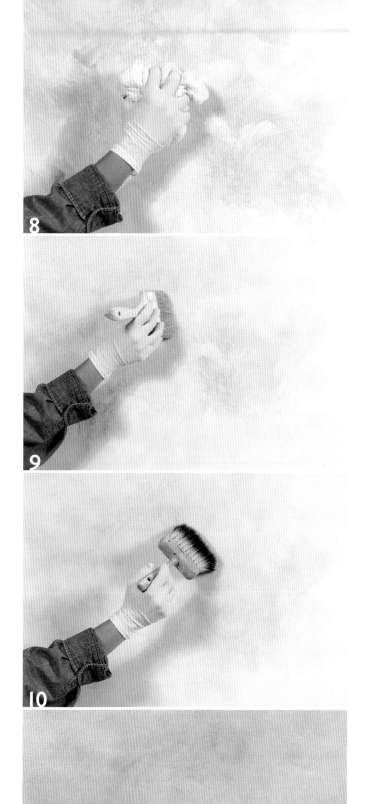

8 Move to the center, where the glaze is still heavy and wet, and pounce outward, stopping short of the edge you created in the previous step.

9 Holding the taped brushes perpendicular to the surface, stipple in a quick tapping motion to blend the glazes.

10 Using just the tips of the blender brush, sweep across the surface in a crisscross or semicircular motion to blend the glazes.

tip DO NOT USE THE SIDE OF THE BLENDER BRUSH OR APPLY TOO MUCH PRESSURE; IF YOU DO, YOU'LL CREATE NOTICE-ABLE LINES. TO MINIMIZE ANY LINES, BLEND LIGHTLY IN THE OPPOSITE DIRECTION.

11 Move to the adjacent area and apply more glaze with the chip brushes.

12 Continue pouncing, stippling, and blending the glaze to complete the walls (see Antique Glazing, Steps 12–16, page 39).

aged walls

This fast-moving, three-layer faux finish mimics the look of time-worn stucco or plaster. Unlike subtractive techniques, which lift the glaze off the wall, this finish involves moving the glaze on the surface to create a haze of color. ◆ *The first layer, a semi-sheer glaze made with bronze paint, creates a foundation for the second layer, a sheer glaze made with universal tints (page 13). The final layer of green and cream accent glazes enhances the aged appearance.*

materials

Basic painting supplies
    (page 8)

Standard roller frame with
    9-inch roller cover

Cheesecloth

One 3-inch chip brush

One 4-inch chip brush

Cream latex paint, satin
    finish, for base coat

Bronze latex paint, satin
    finish, for Layer 1 glaze

Universal tints (page 13)
    in raw umber and burnt
    umber for Layer 2 glaze

Green and cream latex
    paints, satin finish,
    for Layer 3 glazes

Latex glazing liquid

1   Using the standard roller, apply a base coat of cream paint to the walls; allow to dry. Apply a second coat; allow to dry.

2   Mix each paint glaze following this recipe: I part paint to 2 parts glazing liquid. Mix the burnt umber and raw umber universal tint glaze (see "Mixing Glazes," page 16).

layer I

3   Start in the upper area of the wall, near a corner. Using the 3-inch chip brush held almost vertically, apply the bronze glaze generously in a random, downward pattern. Make this pattern large and open; you'll fill in with other glazes in the next two layers.

4   With a flat cheesecloth pom-pom (page 18), pounce the surface. Rotate your wrist as you go, working the glaze downward. Keep the pom-pom in contact with the surface at all times.

5   Feather the glaze outward to soften and enlarge the section.

steps continue >

tip AVOID CREATING VERTICAL "STRIPES" OF COLOR, THE MOST FREQUENT BEGINNER MISTAKE, BY APPLYING THE GLAZE OUTWARD AS WELL AS DOWNWARD.

6 Return to the area where the glaze is still relatively heavy, reload your pom-pom, and continue working the glaze downward and outward.

7 Using the 4-inch chip brush in a quick tapping motion, stipple to soften the glaze and eliminate tiny lines. Don't overblend the glaze, however; you want the finish to have a slightly rough quality.

8 Work around the room with this glaze in the same manner, remembering to push the glaze down *and* out.

tip MAKE SURE THE FIRST LAYER OF GLAZE IS COMPLETELY DRY BEFORE STARTING THE SECOND LAYER; IF IT ISN'T, YOU RISK CREATING BURNS (PAGE 19) WHEN YOU APPLY THE NEXT GLAZE.

layer 2

9 Using the 3-inch chip brush, apply the universal tint glaze over the first layer and the open areas of the base coat. Avoid going over just the first glaze; the goal is to create a new pattern.

10 With a clean pom-pom, work the glaze down and out to feather and blend the color.

11 Using the 4-inch chip brush, stipple to eliminate any remaining lines. Smooth walls require very light stippling; textured walls need more to bring the glaze out of the nooks and crannies and onto the surface.

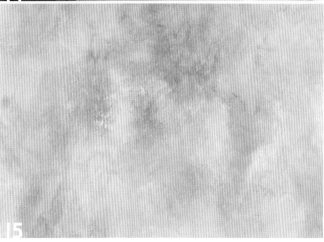

12 Work around the room in the same manner as for Layer 1; allow to dry.

tip STAND BACK AND LOOK AT THE PATTERN AS IT DEVELOPS ON THE WALL. ADD GLAZE TO AREAS AS NEEDED; FOR EXAMPLE, APPLY THE GLAZE LOW ON THE WALL TO BALANCE AN AREA FARTHER UP THE WALL AND TO ONE SIDE.

layer 3

13 Using the 3-inch chip brush, apply small amounts of the green and cream glazes in a random, downward pattern.

14 Using a clean pom-pom, feather and blend the glazes.

15 Work around the room in the same manner; allow to dry.

16 Go back with the universal tint glaze and work across the ceiling and into the corners, pouncing and stippling to create a darker edge. This step visually contains the finish and completes the room.

cloudy skies

A thicker-than-typical mixture of white glaze—equal parts paint and glazing liquid—provides the key to fluffy, fluttery clouds. The shadows are the result of navy blue glaze worked into the lower portion of some clouds. ◆ You can paint your walls in any color you like; these were painted sky blue. You'll need only one quart each of white and navy paint for the glazes.

materials

Basic painting supplies
    (page 8)

Standard roller frame with
    9-inch roller cover

Mini-roller frame with
    6-inch roller cover

Cheesecloth

One 3-inch chip brush for
    stippling

One 2-inch chip brush for
    applying navy glaze

Blender brush

Sky blue latex paint, satin
    finish, for base coat

White latex paint, satin
    finish, for glaze

Navy blue latex paint,
    satin finish, for glaze

Latex glazing liquid

1 Using the standard roller, apply a base coat of sky blue paint to the walls; allow to dry. Apply a second coat; allow to dry.

2 Mix the white glaze following this recipe: I part paint to I part glazing liquid. Mix the navy glaze following this recipe: I part paint to 3 parts glazing liquid (see "Mixing Glazes," page 16).

3 Using the mini-roller, apply the white glaze generously in a loose pattern that approximates a cloud shape.

4 Using a slightly wrinkled cheesecloth pom-pom (page 18), pounce the edges. Rotate your wrist as you go to feather and blend the glaze. Leave the glaze heavier in the center.

5 Holding the 3-inch chip brush perpendicular to the surface, stipple the interior of the cloud in a quick tapping motion to soften the glaze. Using the corner of the brush, stipple outward to "grow" the edges. Leave a white highlight in the center.

6 With the 2-inch chip brush, apply the navy glaze at the lower edge of the cloud. Although dark at first, the glaze will lighten as you work it in.

steps continue >

7 Pounce the navy glaze to blend it into the white glaze.

8 With the 3-inch brush held perpendicular to the surface, stipple the glaze to blend the colors.

9 Using just the tips of the blender brush, sweep across the surface in a semicircular motion to soften the interior of the cloud and make the edges wispy. (Working in a semicircular motion keeps the cloud rounded and creates the illusion that it is moving through the sky.)

10 Repeat the steps to create a smaller cloud to one side. If you make this cloud a bit lighter, it will appear more distant.

tip ADD A LITTLE WHITE GLAZE AT THE EDGES, IF NEEDED, TO FILL OUT THE SHAPE. USE THE POM-POM LOADED WITH WHITE GLAZE TO CREATE A DELICATE CLOUD FLUTTER AT ONE END.

materials

Basic painting supplies
(page 8)

Standard roller frame with
9-inch roller cover

Mini-roller frame with
6-inch roller cover

Cheesecloth

Two 4-inch chip brushes

Masking tape

Red latex paint, satin finish,
for base coat

Chocolate brown latex paint,
satin finish, for glaze

Latex glazing liquid

leather

*Even the novice will find this faux-leather finish surprisingly
doable when worked in sections.* ◆ *A one-color glaze (chocolate brown)
is rolled over a red base coat, then pounced and stippled to a rich visual
texture. A raspberry red, like the color shown here, provides the best base
for the brown glaze. Overlapping the edges of the sections, which is actually
easier to do than blending them, creates the look of "skins."*

technique

1   Using the standard roller, apply a base coat of red paint to the walls; allow to dry. Apply a second coat; allow to dry.

2   Mix the brown glaze following this recipe: I part paint to 2 parts glazing liquid (see "Mixing Glazes," page 16).

3   Tape the chip brushes together with the masking tape; set aside.

4   Using the mini-roller, apply the glaze generously in an irregular, natural shape.

5   Using a flat cheesecloth pom-pom (page 18), pounce the edges. Rotate your wrist as you go to feather the glaze at the edges. For a more distressed leather look, use a wrinkled pom-pom.

6   Rearrange the pom-pom to a clean area of the cheesecloth, and pounce the center area to open up the glaze and reveal more of the base coat.

7   Using the chip brushes in a quick tapping motion, stipple the glaze to create subtle highs (areas of lighter color) and lows (areas of darker color). To lighten the surface even more, lightly pounce the glaze again; then stipple once more to disperse the color.

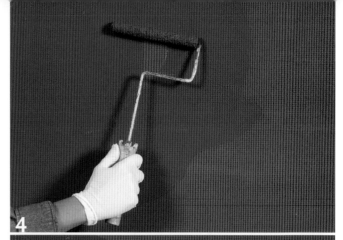

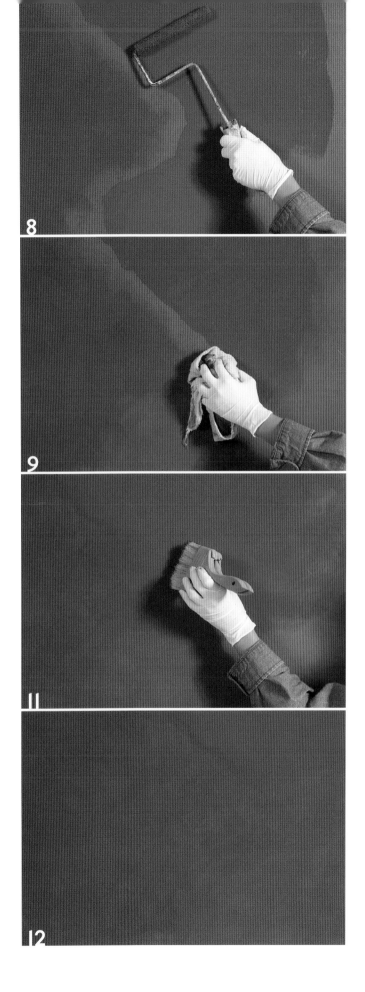

8 Apply the glaze to the adjacent area, rolling close to—but not touching—the edge of the first section. Vary the size and shape of this new section.

9 Pounce the edges to feather the glaze into the first section, slightly overlapping the edges to create the appearance of a seam.

10 Pounce the center area of the section as before.

11 Stipple as before.

12 Continue working in the same manner, section by section, to complete the wall; allow to dry.

13 Work the opposite wall in the same manner; allow to dry. Work the remaining walls.

chamois

Mixing water and glazing liquid with paint gives this tone-on-tone paint treatment a matte, rather than transparent, finish and extends the open time of the glaze. This is a good technique if you're on a limited decorating budget because you blend the glaze using knit rags and cheesecloth instead of a blender brush. ◆ *For the smoothest effect, use all-cotton (not cotton/poly) rags from high-quality T-shirts. If you prefer to work with a color other than tan, be sure the two paints vary in value (page 20) enough to create a slightly mottled effect.*

materials

Basic painting supplies
    (page 8)

Standard roller frame with
    9-inch roller cover

One 4-inch chip brush

Clean knit rags

Cheesecloth

Light tan latex paint, satin
    finish, for base coat

Medium tan latex paint,
    satin finish, for glaze

Latex glazing liquid

1. Using the standard roller, apply a base coat of light tan paint to the walls; allow to dry. Apply a second coat; allow to dry.

2. Mix the medium tan glaze following this recipe: 2 parts paint, 1 part water, and 1 part glazing liquid (see "Mixing Glazes," page 16).

3. Wet the rags and the cheesecloth; wring out the excess moisture and set aside.

4. Begin in the upper area of the wall, near a corner. Using the chip brush, apply the glaze generously in a loose X pattern that's approximately 2 by 2 feet.

5. Using one of the rags, manipulate the glaze on the surface in a light scrubbing motion. Keep the edges soft and irregular. When the rag becomes loaded with glaze, switch to a fresh rag; rinse the rags as needed.

6. Using a slightly wrinkled cheesecloth pom-pom (page 18), pounce to refine the glaze. Rotate your wrist as you go to feather and blend the glaze. Keep the edges soft and irregular. Try to create subtle highs (areas of lighter color) and lows (areas of darker color). Rearrange your pom-pom to a clean area of the cheesecloth as soon as the area you're using becomes loaded with glaze.

7. Apply the glaze to the adjacent area, making sure not to brush too close to the just-completed section.

8. Manipulate the edges with the rag to feather the color toward the first section. Overlap only in the lightest area of the previously created edge. If you stray too far, the color will be darker where the edges overlap.

9. Pounce with the pom-pom to refine the glaze.

10. Continue working in the same manner, section by section, to complete the walls.

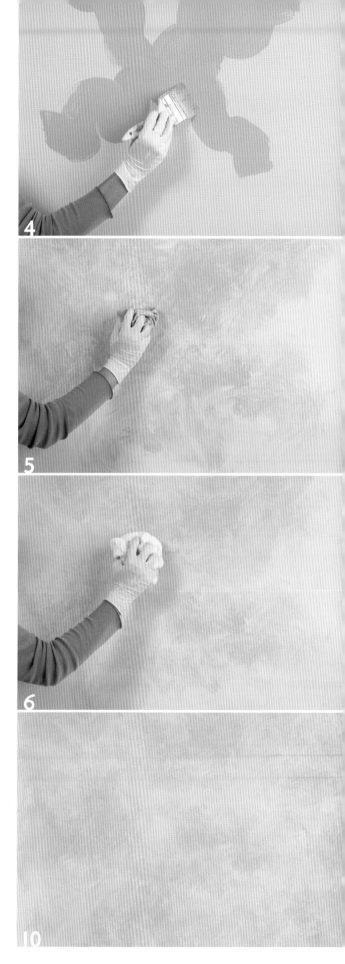

aged bronze

The basic antiquing technique of rolling on a glaze, manipulating it with a cheesecloth pom-pom, then blending it with a blender brush is repeated three times for this luxurious finish.

◆ *Although the process is more time-consuming than a one-color faux finish, the three layers of glaze tend to disguise any irregularities in application, and the depth and richness make the result worth the effort.*

1   Using the standard roller, apply a base coat of cream paint to the walls; allow to dry. Apply a second coat; allow to dry.

2   Mix each glaze following this recipe: I part paint to 2 parts glazing liquid (see "Mixing Glazes," page 16).

3   Begin in the upper area of a wall, near a corner. Using the mini-roller, apply the gold glaze generously in a random, natural pattern that's approximately 2 by 2 feet. Cover the base-coat color with glaze.

4   Using a flat cheesecloth pom-pom (page 18), pounce the edges. Rotate your wrist as you go to feather and blend the glaze. Keep the edges soft and irregular.

5   Rearrange your pom-pom to a clean area of the cheesecloth and pounce the center area in a light scrubbing motion to refine the glaze.

6   Using just the tips of the blender brush, sweep across the surface in a crisscross or semicircular motion to blend the glaze.

steps continue >

tip DO NOT USE THE SIDE OF THE BLENDER BRUSH OR APPLY TOO MUCH PRESSURE; IF YOU DO, YOU'LL CREATE NOTICEABLE LINES. TO MINIMIZE ANY LINES, BLEND LIGHTLY IN THE OPPOSITE DIRECTION.

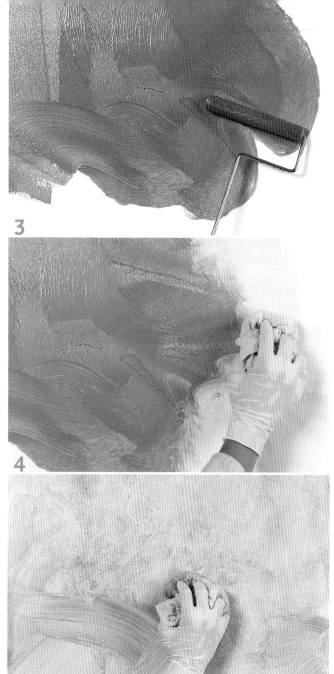

aged bronze | 63

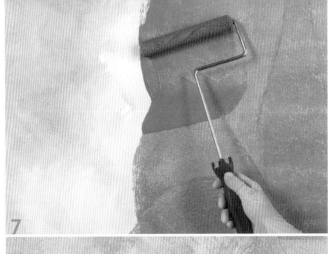

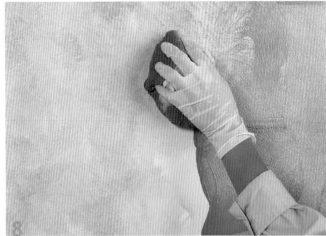

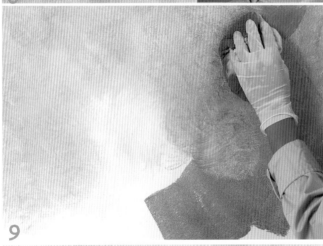

7   Apply the glaze to the adjacent area, making sure not to roll too close to the just-completed section.

8   Pounce the edges to feather the color toward the first section. Overlap only in the lightest area of the previously created edge. If you stray too far into the first section, the color will be darker where the edges overlap.

9   Pounce the center area to refine the glaze.

10 Blend the glaze as before.

11 Continue working in the same manner, section by section, to complete the walls; allow to dry.

tip STAND BACK AND LOOK AT THE PATTERN AS IT DEVELOPS ON THE WALL. ADD GLAZE TO AREAS AS NEEDED; FOR EXAMPLE, APPLY THE GLAZE LOW ON THE WALL TO BALANCE AN AREA FARTHER UP THE WALL AND TO ONE SIDE.

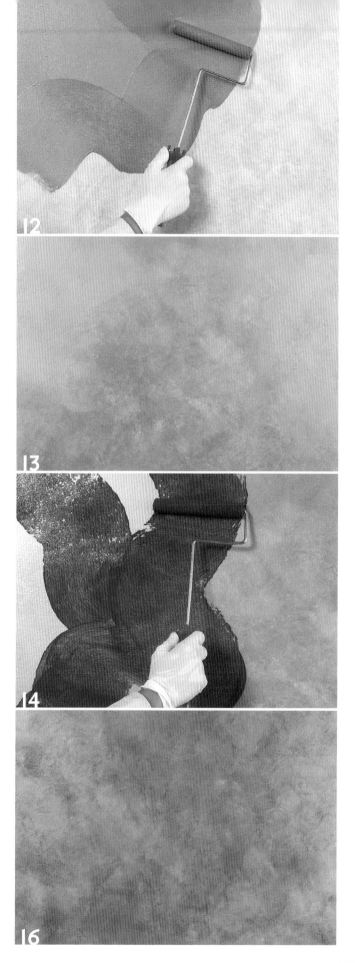

12 Apply the copper glaze as you did the gold glaze.

13 Feather, pounce, and blend the glaze as before with the cheesecloth pom-pom and blender brush to complete the walls; allow to dry.

14 Apply the burnt umber glaze in a random, natural pattern, leaving some of the existing color showing rather than covering the surface.

15 Feather, pounce, and blend the glaze as before.

16 Continue working in the same manner to complete the walls; allow to dry.

porcelain crackle

The technique shown here uses a base coat of glue and a top coat of varnish made specially for crackling. However, you can achieve a similar effect with a one-coat product. ◆ Follow the manufacturer's guidelines for the required room temperature; if you do not, the surface will not crack. With either process, apply a dark commercial antiquing glaze to accentuate the crackling pattern; the glaze color shown here is described as "asphalt."

materials

Basic painting supplies (page 8)

Standard roller frame with 9-inch roller cover

Mini-roller frame with 6-inch roller cover

One 4-inch foam brush

Cheesecloth

Silver latex paint, metallic finish, for base coat

Crackle base coat (glue)

Crackle top coat (varnish)

Commercial antiquing glaze

1   Using the standard roller, apply a base coat of silver paint; allow to dry. Apply a second coat; allow to dry.

tip BECAUSE THIS FINISH CAN BE UNPREDICTABLE, BE SURE TO EXPERIMENT ON A SAMPLE BOARD (PAGE 19).

2   Using the mini-roller, apply the crackle base coat (glue) evenly, feathering the edges where the widths overlap to prevent roller lines; allow to dry according to the manufacturer's instructions.

3   Using the mini-roller, apply the crackle top coat (varnish) evenly; allow to dry according to the manufacturer's instructions.

4   Once the cracks appear, apply the commercial antiquing glaze using the foam brush.

5   Using a flat cheesecloth pom-pom (page 18), rub the glaze in a circular pattern to fill the cracks and darken the surface. Rub off the excess glaze.

6   Continue applying and rubbing the glaze to complete the walls.

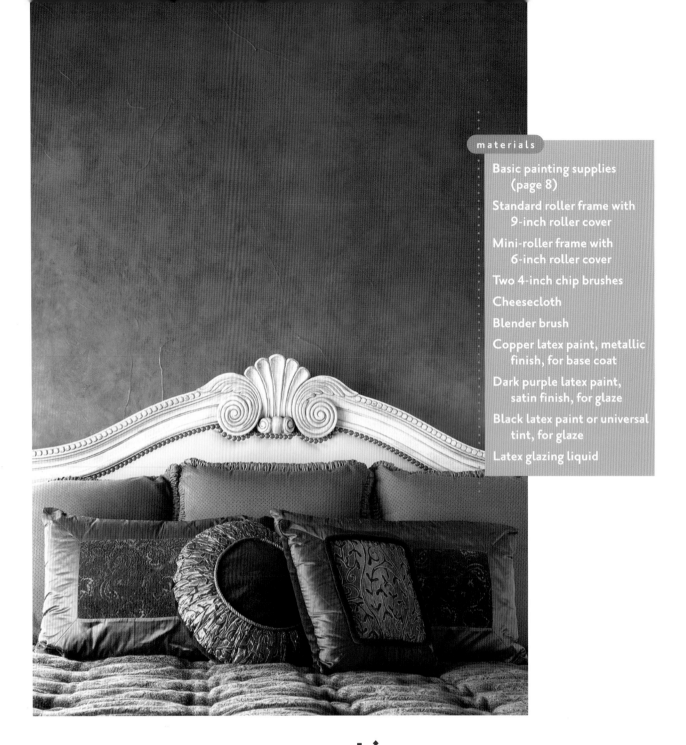

materials

Basic painting supplies
   (page 8)

Standard roller frame with
   9-inch roller cover

Mini-roller frame with
   6-inch roller cover

Two 4-inch chip brushes

Cheesecloth

Blender brush

Copper latex paint, metallic
   finish, for base coat

Dark purple latex paint,
   satin finish, for glaze

Black latex paint or universal
   tint, for glaze

Latex glazing liquid

copper patina
This simple faux finish creates a look of complex color and visual texture using just one glaze worked over a base coat of copper metallic paint. ◆ *For the glaze, choose the deepest purple latex paint available—a color that might be called "eggplant"—and add a little black to darken it. If your room is large, keep the glazing pattern open, as shown here, with plenty of the base-coat color showing through.*

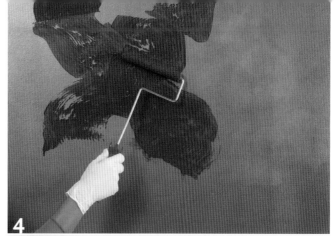

1   Using the standard roller, apply a base coat of copper paint; allow to dry. Apply a second coat; allow to dry.

2   Mix the purple glaze following this recipe: I part paint to 3 parts glazing liquid (see "Mixing Glazes," page 16). Add a small amount of black latex paint or a tiny amount of black universal tint (page 13) to darken the glaze.

3   Tape the chip brushes together using blue painter's tape; set aside.

4   Begin in the upper area of the wall, near a corner. Using the mini-roller, apply the glaze generously in a random, natural pattern that's approximately 2 by 2 feet.

5   Using a slightly wrinkled cheesecloth pom-pom (page 18), pounce the edges. Rotate your wrist as you go to feather and blend the glaze. Keep the edges soft and irregular.

6   Move to the center where the glaze is still heavy and wet, and pounce outward, stopping short of the edge made in the previous step. Try to create subtle highs (areas of lighter color) and lows (areas of darker color).

7   Use the chip brushes in a quick tapping motion to soften the glaze and eliminate tiny lines.

steps continue >

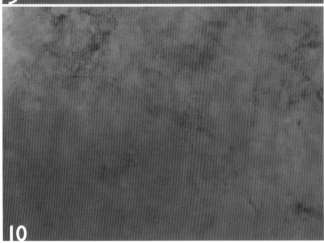

8 Using just the tips of the blender brush, sweep across the surface in a crisscross or semicircular motion to blend the glaze (see Tip, page 38).

9 Apply the glaze to the adjacent area, making sure not to roll too close to the just-completed section.

10 Continue pouncing, stippling, and blending the glaze to complete the walls (see Antique Glazing, Steps 12–16, page 39).

tip AS YOU WORK ADJACENT AREAS, STRIVE TO CREATE THE ILLUSION OF COLOR THAT FLOWS FROM ONE SECTION TO THE NEXT.

venetian plaster

Lustrous and silky smooth, Venetian plaster ranks high among elegant wall finishes. Traditionally, the plaster is applied in thin, multiple layers. However, if you paint your walls first with the same (or a slightly lighter) color as the plaster, you can achieve the desired effect with just two coats. ◆ *The plaster comes ready-mixed in a range of muted colors. This finish requires smooth or very slightly textured walls, so prepare your walls if necessary (or have a professional prepare them).* ◆ *For a more luminous finish, choose a top coat that you can burnish.*

1 Wipe the walls with a terry cloth towel to remove any debris.

2 Using the standard roller, apply a base coat of beige paint to the walls; allow to dry.

3 Sand one edge of each steel spatula, or "spat," to sharpen it (page 11). A sharp edge ensures smooth application of the plaster, which is essential for proper burnishing.

4 Using a kitchen spatula, transfer a small amount of plaster from the can into the trough; replace the can's lid immediately. Begin at the edges—at the ceiling line, above the baseboards, and in the corners. Use your finger to apply a bead of Venetian plaster at the edges, or dilute the plaster with a little water and paint it on using the filbert brush.

5 Scoop a small amount of plaster out of the trough with the 3-inch spat and transfer it to the sanded edge of the 6-inch spat. Put the plaster in the center of the spat, not at the corners. Plaster at the corners will be forced off the ends when you scrape the spat, making tiny lines in the finish.

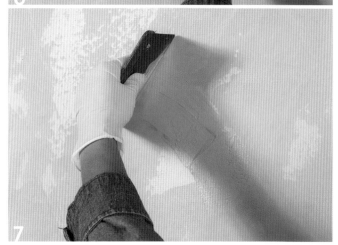

6 With the spat held at a low angle and your fingers near the edge, drag the spat across the wall to apply the plaster.

tip WIPE THE SPATS OCCASIONALLY WITH A CLEAN TERRY CLOTH TOWEL TO PREVENT DRIED BITS OF PLASTER FROM BEING TRANSFERRED TO THE WALL.

7 With the spat held at a high angle, scrape the spat across the plaster you just applied, leaving a thin, smooth layer on the surface.

8 Transfer more plaster to the 6-inch spat and repeat the process, dragging at a low angle to apply the plaster and scraping at a high angle to leave a thin layer. It's not necessary to get complete coverage with the first coat; you'll fill in with a second coat.

9 Work in sections on the wall—high, low, and in between—to complete the first coat. Allow the plaster to dry at least four hours.

10 With the sanded edge of the 6-inch spat toward the wall and the spat held at a low angle, back-burnish the dried plaster by vigorously pushing the edge of the spat forward, against the wall. This step knocks off any nibs of plaster and ensures a smooth second coat. Keep the spat held as flat against the wall as possible.

tip AT THE EDGES AND IN THE CORNERS, YOU MAY FIND IT EASIER TO BACK-BURNISH WITH THE 3-INCH SPAT.

11 Apply a second coat of plaster in the same manner, making sure to cover any spots missed in the first coat.

12 With the spat held at a high angle, scrape the plaster as before.

13 Allow the plaster to dry; then back-burnish. Walk the room and look at each wall carefully to make sure you've covered the entire surface with plaster. Fill in any holes with additional plaster.

14 Apply the acrylic top coat as you did the plaster, dragging it at a low angle and scraping it at a high angle. It's essential to apply the top coat evenly. Allow it to dry according to the manufacturer's instructions; burnish, if appropriate.

venetian plaster diamonds

The challenge of this bold finish is not in applying the Venetian plaster (pages 71–73) but in measuring, marking, and taping off the diamonds. For the best results, enlist the aid of a helper for these preliminary steps. ◆ *Once the walls are taped, the process is much easier than it looks: You tape just once and apply only one layer of the plaster in each color. The diamonds shown in the photo above measure 27 inches wide and 44½ inches high; for clarity, the step-by-step diamonds are half-scale.*

1   Using the standard roller, apply a base coat of beige paint to the walls; allow to dry. Apply a second coat; allow to dry.

measuring and marking

2   Determine the measurements of your diamonds as follows:

- Measure the wall vertically, excluding crown molding (if any) and baseboards, and divide by 2; that's the height of one diamond. It's also the main midpoint on the wall (see the illustration below).

- Measure the wall horizontally and experiment to find a pleasing diamond width that divides evenly into the wall width, such as 24-inch-wide diamonds on a 120-inch-wide wall.

    NOTE: The opposite wall will have identical diamonds because the walls are the same width. On the remaining walls, which will be identical to each other, you may need to adjust the diamond width slightly. Variations up to 1½ inches are not noticeable.

3   Start in the left corner of the first wall. Using the carpenter's level, acrylic rotary ruler, and pencil —and working at the upper edge of the wall, just below the crown molding, if any—measure and mark full diamond widths across the wall. Repeat at the lower edge, just above the baseboard.

4   Starting in the same corner, measure and mark the main midpoint on the wall. From this point measure and mark full diamond widths across the wall, using the level to ensure that you are always at the midpoint. (If you aren't, your diamonds will lean.)

5   Measure and mark a secondary midpoint halfway between the upper edge and the main midpoint. From this secondary midpoint measure and mark a half diamond width; from there, measure and mark full diamond widths across the wall. Repeat between the main midpoint and the lower edge.

6   Repeat Steps 3–5 to mark the opposite wall. Then measure and mark the remaining pair of walls, adjusting the diamond width as needed.

steps continue >

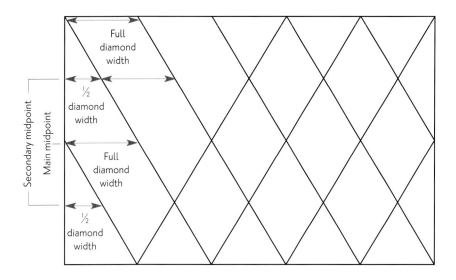

tip REMEMBER THAT PLASTER WILL NOT COVER THE MARKS, SO MAKE THE MARKS ONLY AS HEAVY AS NEEDED TO SEE THEM WHEN YOU APPLY THE TAPE.

taping the diamonds

7 Starting in the upper corner of the first wall, connect the dots with tape. To help you get off to a good start, the first piece of tape goes from the upper left corner to the *second* mark at the lower edge. This piece of tape should intersect the marks you made in Steps 4 and 5.

8 Apply the next piece of tape from the first upper mark to the third lower mark, again intersecting the marks in between. Continue applying the pieces of tape from left to right so they slant in the same direction. Apply partial pieces of tape as needed to complete the wall in this direction.

9 Repeat the process, starting from the upper right corner and working to the left, to complete the diamonds on the first wall. Tape the remaining walls in the same manner.

tip YOU'LL NEED TWO PEOPLE TO TAPE OFF LINES THAT INTERSECT A WINDOW. APPLY EACH PIECE OF TAPE RIGHT OVER THE WINDOW AREA. BREAK THE TAPE IN THE MIDDLE OF THE WINDOW; THEN SMOOTH EACH PIECE FROM THE WALL TOWARD THE WINDOW

10 Using the putty knife, burnish the tape, especially where the pieces intersect.

applying the venetian plaster

11 Decide which diamonds will be olive colored; the alternate diamonds will be red. To prevent mistakes, mark every other diamond with a small piece of blue painter's tape, indicating placement of one of the colors; leave the alternate diamonds unmarked. (The diamonds shown were not marked.)

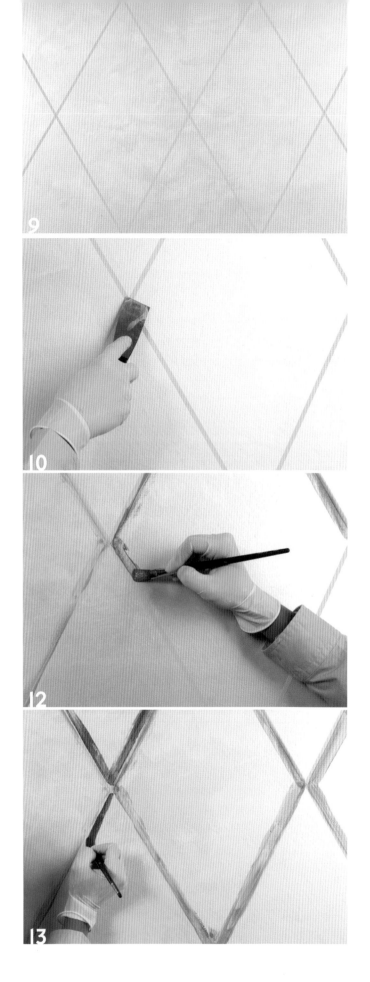

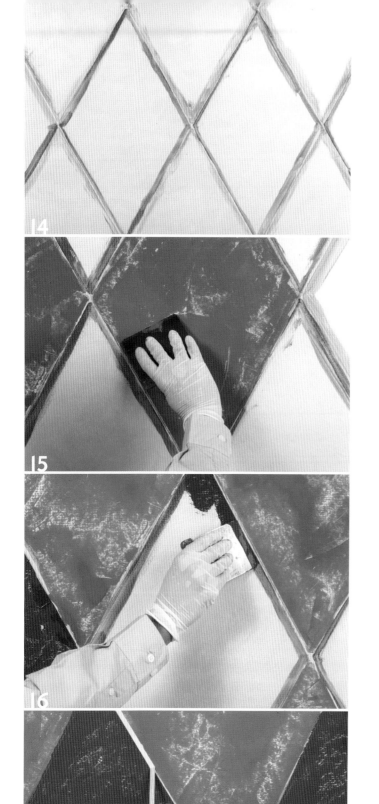

12 Using the artist's round brush, apply a small amount of olive plaster over the edges of the tape and just into the olive diamonds.

13 Repeat with the red plaster in the alternate diamonds.

14 Make sure you have painted all of the edges correctly before proceeding.

15 Read through the general instructions for Venetian plaster, pages 71–73, to get a feel for how to work with the plaster. Using the steel spat, apply the olive plaster to the appropriate diamonds, starting at the edges of the tape and dragging the spat inward at a low angle. This finish uses only one layer of plaster, so apply it a little heavier than you would for a traditional two-layer finish.

tip REMEMBER TO DRAG THE PLASTER WITH THE SPAT HELD AT A LOW ANGLE; THEN SCRAPE THE PLASTER WITH THE SPAT HELD AT A HIGH ANGLE.

16 Repeat with the red plaster.

17 Allow the plaster to dry according to the manufacturer's instructions. Slowly pull the tape, starting with the pieces on top.

18 Repeat on the remaining walls to complete the room.

19 Apply the top coat (see Step 14, page 73).

powder pigments

Venetian plaster serves as the base for the ethereal finish shown here, but you can also start with painted walls. The key ingredients, powder pigments, available through art supply sources, are concentrated colored powders without binders. A little powder pigment goes a long way: For an entire room, it takes only 1 teaspoon of powder to 1 cup of water for each of the four colors. To preserve the color, you must seal the walls.

materials

Basic painting supplies (page 8)

Venetian Plaster materials (page 71), with the exception of the top coat

Powder pigments: yellow oxide, raw umber, green, and blue

Four small, shallow containers for mixing powder pigments

Sea sponge to apply color

Cellulose sponge to rub color

Clear acrylic sealer, matte finish

Mini-roller frame with 6-inch roller cover (¼-inch nap) to apply sealer

MONET

RENOIR

1 Follow Steps 1–13 for Venetian Plaster, pages 71–73, to apply the plaster to the walls. Do not apply a top coat.

2 For each color, mix 1 teaspoon of the powder pigment and 1 cup of water in a shallow plastic container.

3 Dip the sea sponge into one or more of the colors—yellow oxide and raw umber in this example—and quickly apply a thin wash of color to the wall.

4 Move the color over the surface rapidly with the sponge. Wipe away any drips as you go. (They will show later if left.)

5 Apply a wash of green, blending it with the yellow and umber.

6 Follow with a wash of blue as an accent.

steps continue >

tip BE VERY CAREFUL WITH THE WALLS AT THIS POINT BECAUSE THE COLOR IS NOT SET OR SEALED.

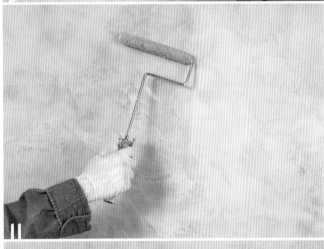

7 Allow the walls to dry thoroughly, at least 1 hour.

8 Using the cellulose sponge in a back-and-forth rubbing motion, work off some of the pigment. (The sponge shown here appears dark because it is backed with a scouring pad.) At first it takes only light pressure to pick up the color. As the sponge begins to fill with pigment, you'll need to use more pressure. Don't rub in circles or you will create holes in the color.

tip IF YOU ACCIDENTALLY CREATE A HOLE IN THE COLOR, USE THE SEA SPONGE TO FILL IN WITH PIGMENT. ALLOW THE AREA TO DRY; THEN WORK IT WITH THE CELLULOSE SPONGE AS BEFORE.

9 When it becomes difficult to remove pigment, rinse the sponge and wring out almost all of the moisture. Move to an area of heavy color and continue rubbing off pigment until you reach the desired color. (If you return to an area you've already worked, the damp sponge will remove too much pigment.)

10 Continue working in the same manner, section by section, to complete the walls.

11 Stir the sealer thoroughly. Using the mini-roller, apply the matte acrylic sealer evenly.

12 Allow the sealer to dry. Don't be concerned about roller lines; they will disappear.

stone blocks

Venetian plaster and powder pigments combine to create a weathered stone wall. ◆ *Read the introduction to Venetian Plaster on page 71 and Powder Pigments on page 78 before you undertake this project. You can apply powder pigments over a base coat of latex paint, rather than the plaster, for a softer, less textured effect. Work out the block pattern on paper, fitting it to your wall dimensions, before you measure and mark.*

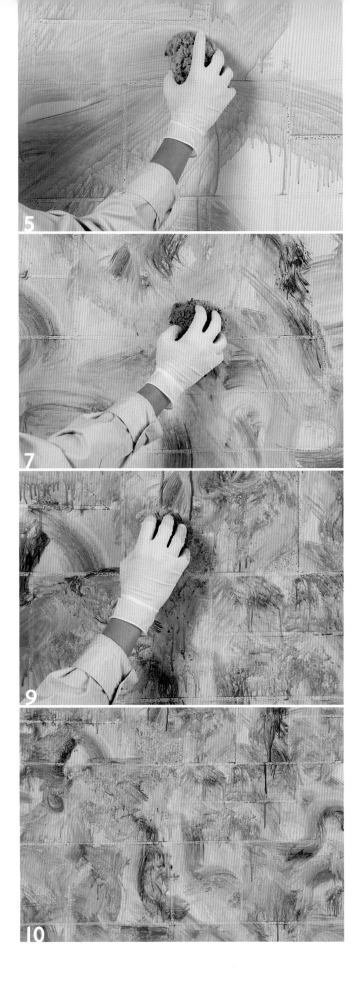

technique

1 Follow Steps 1–13, pages 71–73, to apply the plaster to the walls.

2 Using the carpenter's level (page 9), straightedge, and pencil, lightly draw the block pattern on the wall.

3 Before you tape the pattern, decide whether you will place the tape above or below, to the right or left, of the marked lines. Being consistent with the placement, tape off the design using the masking tape. Leave small tabs of tape on the ends to make removal easier.

4 For each color, mix 1 teaspoon of the powder pigment and 1 cup of water in a shallow plastic container.

5 Dip the sea sponge into the gray mixture and quickly apply a thin wash of color to the wall.

6 Move the color over the surface rapidly with the sponge, wiping away any drips as you go. (They will show later if left.)

7 Apply a wash of burnt umber, blending it with the gray.

8 Apply a wash of raw umber, blending it with the gray and burnt umber.

9 Finish with a wash of green, blending it with the other three colors.

10 Allow the walls to dry thoroughly, at least 1 hour.

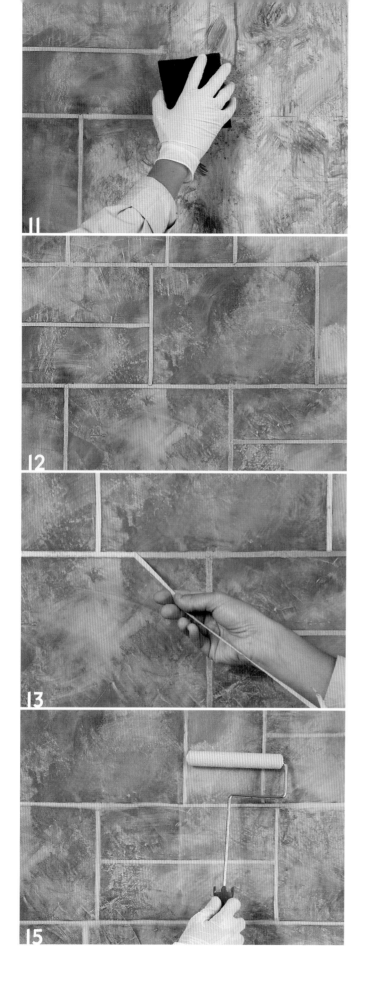

tip BE VERY CAREFUL WITH THE WALLS AT THIS POINT; THE COLOR IS NOT SET OR SEALED.

11 Follow Step 8, page 80, to work off some of the color.

12 Continue working off the color (follow Step 9, page 80).

13 Remove the tape. Don't be concerned if some of the color has seeped under the edges; it adds to the weathered look and softens the lines.

14 If desired, lightly feather some of the color into the "grout lines" using the cellulose sponge.

15 Stir the sealer thoroughly. Using the mini-roller, apply the matte acrylic sealer evenly. Don't be concerned about roller lines; they will disappear as the sealer dries.

materials

Basic painting supplies
(page 8)

Plumb bob and pencil
(optional; see Step 2)

Standard roller frame with
9-inch roller cover

Mini-roller frame with
6-inch roller cover

Clean terry cloth towel

One 4-inch chip brush

Ivory latex paint, satin
finish, for base coat

Willow green latex paint,
satin finish, for glaze

Latex glazing liquid

strié
Elegant and understated, a strié finish requires patience and a steady hand. ◆ *Because you must step up and down to drag the brush through the glaze, it's best done in a room with 8-foot ceilings, where you can use a step stool instead of a ladder.* ◆ *To ensure straight up-and-down lines, stand directly in front of the wall when you roll and drag the glaze. This faux finish takes practice, so experiment first on a board, then on your wall, wiping off the glaze quickly.*

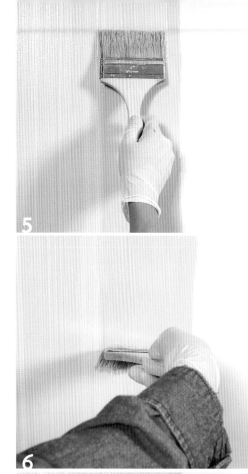

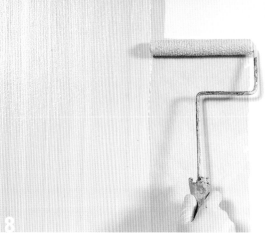

1   Using the standard roller, apply a base coat of ivory paint to the walls; allow to dry. Apply a second coat; allow to dry.

2   If you're not confident you can keep the strié pattern from leaning, use a plumb bob and pencil to mark faint lines every 3 feet. Follow these lines to keep your brush moving straight down the wall.

3   Mix the glaze following this recipe: I part paint to 2 parts glazing liquid (see "Mixing Glazes," page I6).

4   Stand directly in front of the wall, near a corner. Using the mini-roller and starting halfway up the wall, roll the glaze as close to the ceiling as possible. Immediately roll back to the center and down to the baseboard. Roll again from the ceiling all the way down to smooth out the glaze. Roll a second width of glaze in the same manner, barely covering the edge of the first width.

5   Position the step stool directly in front of the rolled glaze and step up. Working with the side of the chip brush, push the glaze to the ceiling; then immediately drag the bristles down through the glaze. When you have gone as far as you can without stepping down, lift the brush lightly, feathering out the tiny lines.

6   Step down, move the stool to the side, and bend your knees so you can work from the bottom up. Flip the brush to the clean side, push the glaze to the baseboard, and drag up. As you approach the point where you stopped in the previous step, lift the brush lightly, feathering the tiny lines.

7   Discharge the paint from the chip brush completely, using the terry cloth towel. (If you don't, the brush will load up with paint and you'll lose the strié effect.) Drag the second width in the same manner, overlapping the edge of the first width a little and leaving a I-inch wet edge (see page I9).

8   Roll on the next two widths of glaze, just overlapping the wet edge but not touching the strié pattern.

9   Drag the glaze, feathering your strokes at a different point on the wall and overlapping each previously dragged width.

10 Continue rolling and dragging the glaze to complete the wall; allow to dry.

11 Work the opposite wall in the same manner; allow to dry. Work the remaining walls.

strié stripes

Crisp stripes and soft strié combine in this tailored wall finish. Blue painter's tape in two widths makes quick work of taping off the stripes and spaces. ◆ The instructions describe how to roll and drag each of the three colors, but you can do several stripes of the same color and then shift gears and work with the next color. Wrap the brushes tightly in plastic when not using them to prevent the paint from drying in the bristles.

materials

Basic painting supplies
(page 8)

Carpenter's level

One 6- by 24-inch acrylic
rotary ruler (page 9)

Pencil

Blue painter's tape, 1 inch
wide and 2 inches wide

Putty knife

Standard roller frame with
9-inch roller cover

Mini-roller frame with
6-inch roller cover

Trim roller with 3-inch
roller cover

Two 3-inch chip brushes

One 2-inch chip brush

One 1-inch chip brush

Cream latex paint, satin
finish, for base coat

Camel, charcoal, and white
latex paint, satin finish,
for glazes

Latex glazing liquid

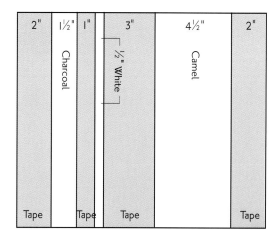

2"	1½"	1"	3"	4½"	2"
	Charcoal		½" White	Camel	
Tape	Tape		Tape		Tape

1. Using the standard roller, apply a base coat of cream paint to the walls; allow to dry. Apply a second coat; allow to dry.

2. Using the carpenter's level, acrylic rotary ruler, and pencil, measure and lightly mark the stripes and spaces on the walls. See the illustration at right for the stripe and space widths shown here. When you reach the first corner, wrap the stripe or space onto the adjacent wall. As you reach the starting corner, adjust the width of the final stripes and spaces; small differences will not be noticeable.

   If you prefer to have a stripe or space end at each corner, measure your walls and work out a pattern of stripes and spaces that fits one wall; the opposite wall will be identical. On the other pair of walls, fudge the stripes and spaces as needed.

3. Tape off the walls using the 1- and 2-inch blue painter's tape to create the spaces. For the 3-inch spaces, combine the 1- and 2-inch tape. Remember, the tape covers the spaces, which will remain the base-coat color. You'll paint the exposed areas camel, charcoal, and white. Burnish the edges of the tape firmly with the putty knife.

4. Mix each of the glazes following this recipe: 1 part paint to 3 parts glazing liquid (see "Mixing Glazes," page 16).

5. Using the mini-roller, apply the camel glaze to the first 4½-inch-wide stripe, rolling just over the edges of the tape.

6. Using a 3-inch chip brush, drag the glaze (see Strié, Steps 5–7, page 85, for dragging instructions).

7. Using the trim roller, apply the charcoal glaze to the first 1½-inch-wide stripe, rolling just over the edges of the tape. Drag the glaze with the clean 3-inch chip brush.

8. Using the 1-inch chip brush, apply the white glaze over the first ½-inch stripe, brushing just over the edges of the tape. Drag the glaze with the 2-inch chip brush.

9. Continue rolling and dragging the stripes to complete the room. Remove the tape.

plaid

This casual paint finish is "subtractive"—that is, you roll on the glaze over a base coat, then drag the surface with a tool to reveal a pattern. ◆ White accent stripes are painted on once the glaze is dry. You'll make your own tools using shower squeegees. Look for ones with the deepest possible blades; if the blades are shallow, the ends may mar the glaze as you drag through it. ◆ The pattern shown here was based on a grid 18 by 24 inches, but you can alter the proportions to suit your room.

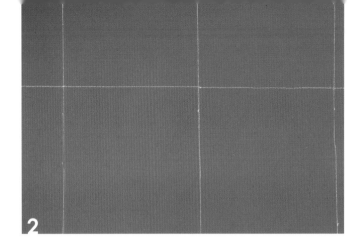

1. Using the standard roller, apply a base coat of blue-green paint; allow to dry.

2. Using the carpenter's level (page 9), straightedge, and chalk, mark a grid 18 inches wide and 24 inches long around the room. The lines need not be perfect; they are a general guide for dragging the squeegees. At the ceiling and baseboard, apply small pieces of tape where the lines begin and end.

3. Mix the camel and white glazes following this recipe: 1 part paint to 2 parts glazing liquid (see "Mixing Glazes," page 16).

4. Cut one squeegee with teeth spaced as shown, for the vertical lines. Cut the remaining squeegee with teeth spaced as shown for the horizontal lines.

5. Using the chip brush, cut in with the camel glaze at the corner. At the ceiling and base-board, cut in 6 to 8 inches beyond the first vertical chalk line.

6. Begin in one corner of the wall. Using the mini-roller, apply enough widths of the camel glaze to equal the distance you cut in at the ceiling and baseboard. Strive for an even distribution of glaze, but allow bits of the base-coat color to show.

7. Stand directly in front of the wall. Using the tape marks as a guide, drag the first vertical lines with the narrow-toothed squeegee from the ceiling to the baseboard. Discharge the accumulated paint on a terry cloth towel.

steps continue >

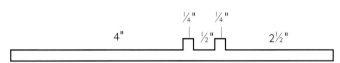

NARROW-TOOTHED SQUEEGEE FOR VERTICAL LINES

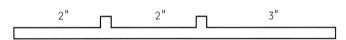

WIDE-TOOTHED SQUEEGEE FOR HORIZONTAL LINES

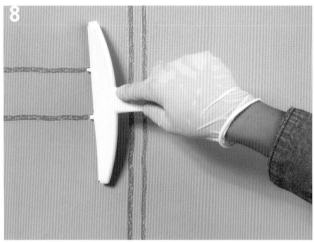

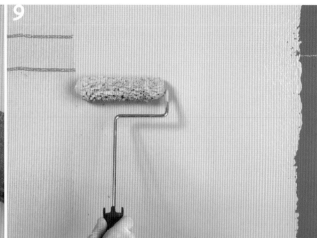

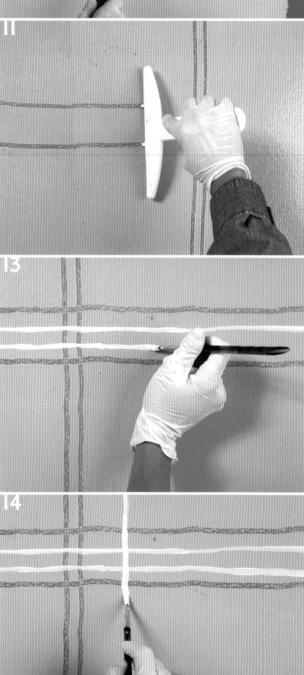

8 Using the horizontal chalk lines as a guide, drag the horizontal lines with the wide-toothed squeegee. Repeat for the remaining horizontal lines.

9 Apply additional widths of camel glaze, rolling over the wet edge of the first section, to cover the next vertical chalk line.

10 Drag the next vertical lines.

11 Starting where you left off, continue dragging the horizontal lines.

12 Continue working across the wall, rolling on the paint and dragging the vertical and horizontal lines; allow to dry. Repeat on the remaining walls to complete the room.

13 Using the white paint and the artist's brush, paint the horizontal accent stripes. Twirl the loaded brush as you move it to apply the paint evenly.

14 Paint the vertical accent stripes.

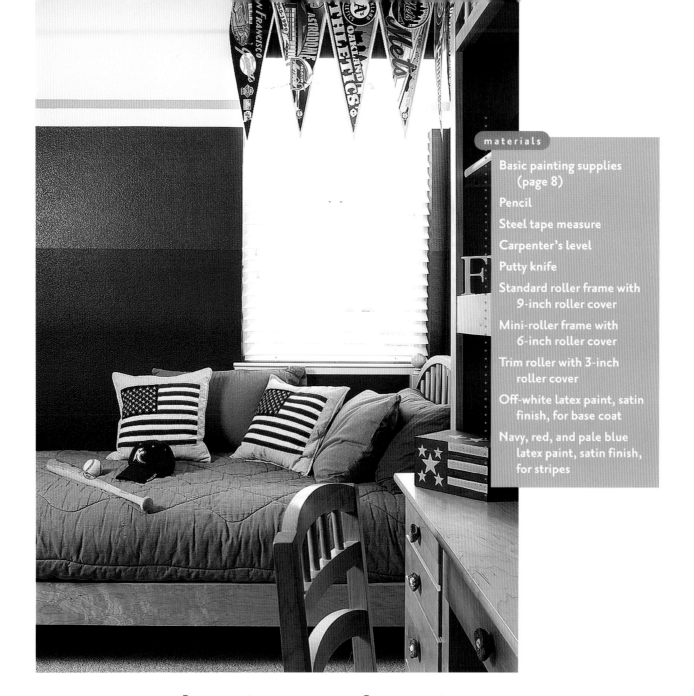

horizontal stripes

Painter's tape is the secret to crisp, clean stripes. ◆ *In this project you'll use a professional technique to prevent the paint from seeping under the tape, ensuring a perfect line—even on slightly textured walls.* ◆ *The stripes in this room range from a 20-inch navy stripe to a 1¼-inch pale blue stripe, but you can alter the widths to suit your room. You'll probably need only one quart of each color, except for the base coat.*

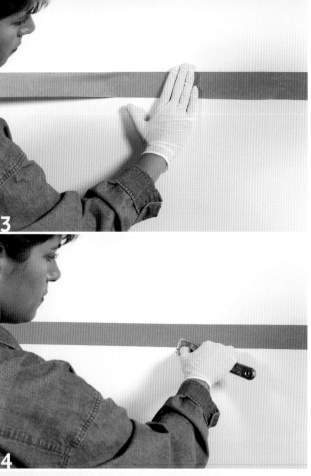

1   Using the standard roller, apply a base coat of off-white paint to the walls; allow to dry. Apply a second coat; allow to dry.

2   Measure and lightly mark horizontal lines on the wall using the steel tape and carpenter's level. The stripes shown on page 91 measure as follows:
      20 inches for the navy stripe
      12 inches for the red stripe
      2 inches for the off-white space
      1¼ inches for the pale blue stripe

3   Tape the navy stripe first. Position the edge of the tape on the 20-inch line, with the tape itself above the line.

4   Using the putty knife, burnish only the edge of the tape that you will paint—in this example, the lower edge.

5   Using the mini-roller, apply the navy paint, rolling just over the burnished edge of the tape; allow the paint to dry. Apply a second coat, if necessary; allow to dry completely.

6   Pull off the tape slowly and gently at a 45-degree angle.

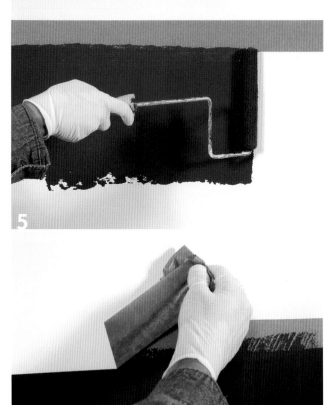

7

to be painted pale blue

to be painted red

8

9

7 To tape the red stripe, position the edge of the tape just a hair below the edge of the navy paint line, with the tape itself in the navy stripe. Burnish the edge that you will paint—in this example, the upper edge.

8 Working up, tape the 2-inch space between the red stripe and the pale blue stripe. Because the tape is 2 inches wide, it will seal both edges of the space at the same time. Also tape the upper edge of the pale blue stripe. (If you are confused about where the tape goes, see the photo in Step 12.)

9 To prevent seepage of the red or pale blue paint under the tape's edges and into the off-white areas, roll over the edges to be painted using the trim roller and the off-white paint; allow to dry.

10 Using the trim roller, paint the pale blue stripe; allow to dry. Apply a second coat, if necessary; allow to dry.

11 Using the mini-roller, paint the red stripe; allow to dry. Apply a second coat; allow to dry.

12 Gently remove the tape.

13 Tape and paint the remaining walls in the same manner to complete the room; allow to dry.

12

materials

- Basic painting supplies (page 8)
- Standard roller frame with 9-inch roller cover
- One 6- by 24-inch acrylic rotary ruler (page 9)
- Carpenter's level
- Light taupe colored pencil
- Small roller frame with 4-inch roller cover
- One 2-inch synthetic paintbrush
- Off-white latex paint, satin finish, for base coat
- Plastic spackling tool
- Light taupe latex paint, satin finish, for stripes
- Blue painter's tape, 1 inch wide
- Pearl opalescent paint
- Plastic plate
- Heavy plastic wrap
- Paper towels

opalescent stripes

Stripes painted off-white and taupe, then dabbed with pearl-toned paint, create an elegant, understated finish. Pay careful attention to which stripes you are taping off in Step 5; it's easy to make a mistake. ◆ *This technique is best suited to smooth walls, but you can still use it if you have textured walls; the opalescent paint will conceal any imperfections in the stripe edges.*

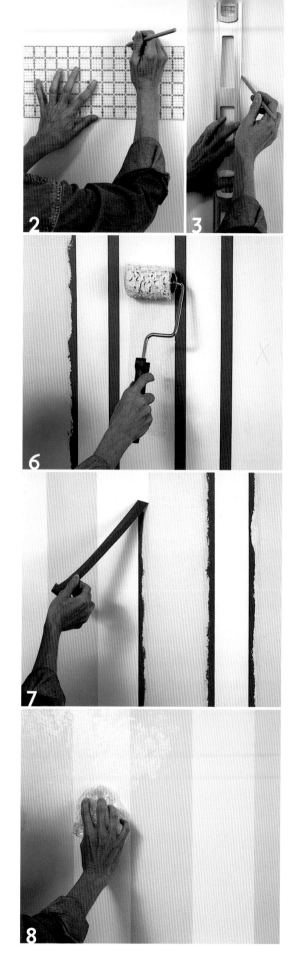

1 Using the standard roller, apply a base coat of off-white paint; allow to dry. Apply a second coat; allow to dry.

2 Starting in a prominent corner, measure and mark 5-inch intervals using the rotary ruler and colored pencil.

3 Using the carpenter's level, draw parallel lines down the wall at the marks you just made, making sure the lines are straight.

4 Lightly mark an X with the colored pencil in every other stripe. These will be the stripes you paint light taupe.

5 Tape the stripes in preparation for painting as follows: Place 1-inch painter's tape in the blank stripes, with the edges precisely on the marked lines. (These stripes will appear narrower than 5 inches because of the tape.) Using the plastic spackling tool, burnish the edges of the tape that are on the lines.

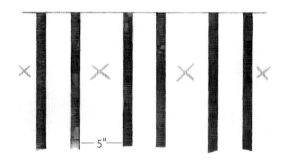

6 Using the small roller with roller cover, paint the X-marked stripes light taupe, rolling just over the edges of the tape.

7 When the paint is dry to the touch, gently pull off the tape at a 45-degree angle. Allow to dry overnight.

8 Pour approximately ½ cup of the opalescent paint onto the plastic plate. Crumple a piece of the plastic wrap. Dip the wrap into the paint, blot on paper towels, and pounce (dab) the wall, rotating your wrist as you go for a random effect. Continue working in the same manner to complete the walls; allow to dry.

one-color fresco

This simple technique, reminiscent of Italian fresco, uses mixtures of universal tint and joint compound to add mottled color and subtle texture to plain walls. On the practical side, this treatment camouflages damaged surfaces and is easy to apply, even for beginners. (If you're new to decorative paint techniques, enlist a friend's help to make the job go faster.)

materials

- Basic painting supplies (page 8)
- Universal tint in yellow oxide
- Latex primer
- Standard roller frame with 9-inch roller cover
- Two 2-gallon buckets with lids
- One 12-pound bucket of wallboard joint compound
- One metal taping knife
- Cellulose sponges
- Spray bottle with a fine-mist nozzle
- Mini-roller frame with 6-inch roller cover
- Clear acrylic sealer, matte finish

96

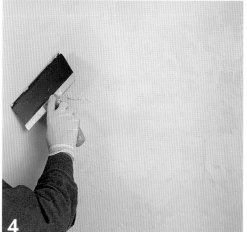

technique

1   Tint the primer with the yellow oxide universal tint to obtain a lighter version of the color you desire. (Your paint source can also tint the primer for you.)

2   Using the standard roller, prime the surface with the tinted primer; allow to dry.

3   Using the universal tint, mix two different-colored batches of the joint compound in the 2-gallon buckets, varying the value (the lightness or darkness) of the colors as desired. If necessary, add a small amount of water to the compound to make it the consistency of spreadable cake frosting.

4   Skim a coat of the lighter compound onto the wall with the taping knife, working in different directions and overlapping your strokes. Strive to get the compound off the knife and onto the wall, rather than just scraping it across the surface. Alternate with the darker compound. Work in a small area and then move to the next area, until the walls are covered.

5   The room will become humid as the compound dries, so open windows and doors and set up fans to speed drying and vent the fumes.

6   Using a damp sponge and a wiping action, smooth and manipulate the compound until you create a slightly raised surface. If the mixture has dried too much to move, spray the surface with a fine mist of water and gently work it with the sponge.

7   Allow the surface to dry thoroughly. Temperature and humidity will affect the drying time of the compound; thicker areas will take considerably longer to dry.

8   Using the mini-roller, apply the matte acrylic sealer; allow to dry.

tip ONCE YOU START WORKING WITH THE COMPOUND, KEEP SCRAPING THE INSIDES OF THE BUCKETS CLEAN. IF YOU DON'T, DRY CHUNKS OF COMPOUND WILL FALL INTO THEM, CAUSING STREAKS WHEN YOU PAINT. WHEN YOU'RE NOT USING THE COMPOUND, SPRAY THE SURFACE OF IT WITH A FINE MIST OF WATER, COVER WITH PLASTIC WRAP, AND REPLACE THE LIDS.

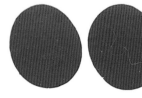

terra fresco
Large rooms can accommodate
the dramatic color and strong visual texture of this bold finish.
◆ You'll mix the joint compound and the paint lightly in a plaster trough, but most of the blending occurs when you spread the
compound across the wall. The ratio of paint to compound deter-
mines the finished look; in the photos shown here, the mixture
was approximately half paint and half compound.

1 The room will become humid as the compound dries. Before you begin, open windows and doors and set up fans to speed drying and vent the fumes.

2 Transfer some of the joint compound from the container to the trough; close the container. Add some of each paint color to the trough and mix lightly with a stir stick. Do not mix completely; you should see all three paint colors distinctly in the trough.

3 Using the taping knife, scoop out some of the mixture from the trough and begin to apply it to the wall.

4 Drag and spread the mixture in a mostly vertical pattern, with some variation in the angle of your strokes.

5 Continue to work the mixture on the wall, being careful not to overblend. Remember that the more you use the taping knife, the more blended the color becomes.

6 As you work your way across the walls, stand back periodically to check the balance of color and texture. If necessary, apply more mixture to certain areas.

7 Continue applying the mixture to complete the walls; allow to dry overnight.

8 Using the mini-roller, apply the matte acrylic sealer; allow to dry.

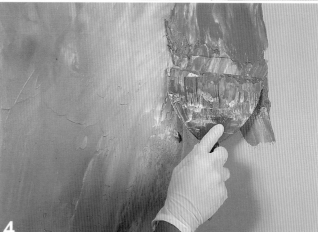

materials

Basic painting supplies
(page 8)

One 4-inch synthetic
paintbrush

All-purpose wallpaper paste

White tissue paper totaling
the square footage of the
walls, plus 10 percent

Latex primer

Latex paint, satin finish, for
base coat and "shadow"
color

Latex glazing liquid

One 2½-inch synthetic
paintbrush

Tile sponge

Clean knit rag

sharpei

White tissue paper and wallpaper paste are the secret ingredients in this simple finish. The crinkly effect comes from manipulating the tissue on the walls while the paste is still wet. Choosing the paint colors is a snap: Select a color for the light base coat, and then count down two hues on the same paint strip for a slightly darker "shadow" color. See pages 26–27 for a dramatic version of this technique.

1 Using the 4-inch brush, apply a thin coat of wallpaper paste over an area slightly larger than one piece of the tissue paper.

tip IF YOU CAN'T SEE THE PASTE ON THE WALLS, SHINE A LIGHT ON IT FROM THE SIDE; THE WET PASTE WILL GLISTEN.

2 Loosely place the first piece of tissue over the pasted area, keeping it approximately straight.

3 As you adhere the tissue to the wall, manipulate it with your hands to create tiny wrinkles. Don't be concerned if the tissue tears; blend any torn edges with additional wallpaper paste.

4 Brush on more paste adjacent to the first sheet. Adhere the second piece, overlapping the first sheet by approximately 1½ inches.

5 Where a noticeable wrinkle occurs in the first sheet of tissue, sculpt the second sheet with your hands so the wrinkle appears to continue across the seam.

6 Brush paste lightly over the seam, following the wrinkles.

7 Continue pasting sheets of tissue paper until the walls are covered; allow to dry overnight.

steps continue >

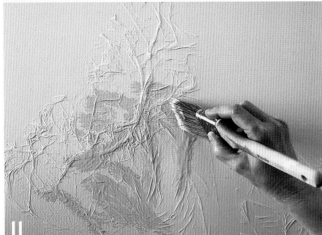

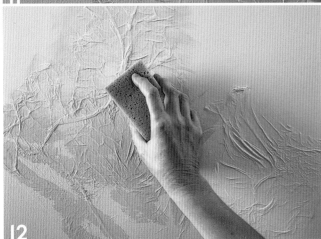

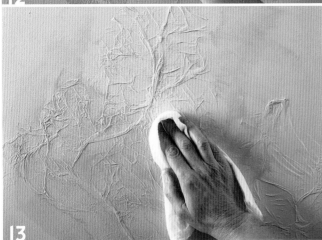

8   Using the 4-inch brush, prime the walls with the latex primer. Work in the direction of the wrinkles, being careful not to let the primer pool in the creases of the tissue; allow the primer to dry.

9   With a minimum of the lighter paint on the brush, paint the walls, brushing in the direction of the wrinkles and being careful not to let the paint pool in the creases; allow to dry.

10   Combine approximately ½ cup of the darker paint and 1 cup of the glazing liquid in a plastic container to make the glaze.

11   Using the 2½-inch brush, dab the glaze over the wrinkles. Work in an area 2 by 2 feet; then proceed immediately to the next step.

12   Moisten the tile sponge and wring it nearly dry. Lightly wipe the painted area with the sponge in a sweeping motion, striving to lift some of the darker paint off the ridges of the wrinkles, while keeping some in the creases to create "shadows." Avoid creating conspicuous stop-and-start lines.

13   Using the cloth, dampened slightly, quickly lift a little of the darker color from the flat areas, blending it toward the wrinkles. Rinse the cloth often; replace as needed.

14   Continue working in the same manner to complete the walls, mixing more glaze as needed.

papier collé

French for paper collage, this tactile finish relies on the use of inexpensive kraft paper (available at framing and art supply stores) and wallpaper paste to create the look and feel of antiquity. ◆ You'll begin at the edges of each wall—at the ceiling line, above the baseboard, and in the corners—and then fill in the remaining areas. Plain glazing liquid seals the walls in preparation for the three colors of glaze. ◆ You can use this finish if your walls are textured, but you will achieve a less dramatic effect. In a bathroom, use a clear acrylic sealer to protect the walls from moisture.

materials

Basic painting supplies
(page 8)

Kraft paper to total square
footage of walls, plus
20 percent

Heavy-duty wallpaper paste

Mini-roller frame with 6-inch
roller cover

One 6-inch foam brayer

One 1-inch chip brush

One 3-inch chip brush

Cheesecloth

Cream, tan, and green latex
paint, satin finish, for
glazes

Latex glazing liquid

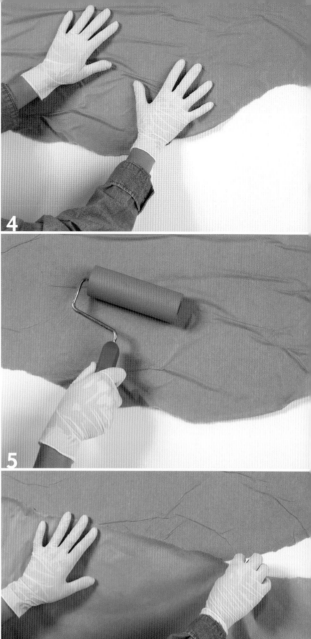

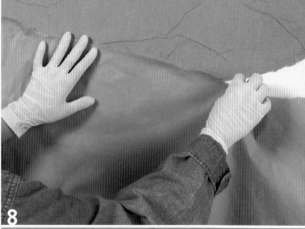

1   Maintaining one straight edge, tear several lengthwise pieces of kraft paper, each approximately 14 inches wide and 3 to 4 feet long.

tip IN GENERAL, TEAR THE PIECES AS LARGE AS YOU CAN MANAGE TO MINIMIZE SEAMS, WHICH TEND TO DISTRACT FROM THE CREASES. FEWER LARGE PIECES HAVE A GREATER VISUAL IMPACT THAN MANY SMALL ONES.

2   Spread the drop cloth on your work surface, and lay the first torn piece on the cloth. Pour wallpaper paste into the paint tray. Using the mini-roller, apply paste to the paper in a forward motion only, not back and forth. Be sure to roll the paste beyond the edges to completely coat the paper.

3   Apply paste to the wall over an area slightly larger than the piece of paper.

4   Adhere the paper to the upper area of the wall, with the straight edge neatly at the ceiling line. Wrinkle the paper with both hands to create creases; they may be pronounced or subtle, depending on the look you want to achieve.

5   Using the brayer and working from the center out, roll over the surface firmly to flatten the creases and push the air out from under the paper. Make sure you roll a little beyond the edges of the paper to coat them completely; wipe any paste off the brayer with a damp rag. Use your fingers to work out any remaining air bubbles.

6   Stand back and look at the piece carefully to make sure the edges and wrinkles are flat.

7   Tear the next piece of paper in an irregular shape to over-lap the edge of the first piece. Apply paste to the back of the paper and to the wall.

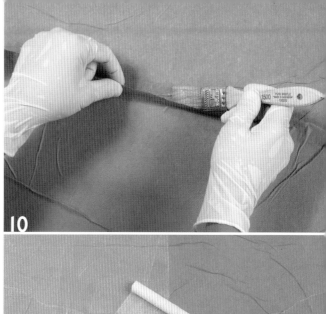

tip OVERLAP THE PIECES AS LITTLE AS POSSIBLE
TO AVOID BULK. IT'S FINE TO TEAR AWAY A
LITTLE OF THE PAPER, IF NECESSARY, WHILE
THE PASTE IS STILL WET.

8   Adhere the piece to the wall, just overlapping the edge
    of the first piece.

9   Wrinkle the paper to create creases.

10 If the edge of the second piece does not stick to the
    first piece, lift the edge and apply a small amount of paste
    with the 1-inch chip brush.

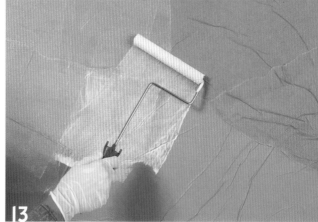

11 Roll over the surface with the brayer.

12 Continue to tear, glue, and adhere pieces of paper to
    complete the wall. Repeat on the remaining walls; allow
    to dry overnight.

13 Using the mini-roller, apply plain glazing liquid over the
    paper to seal the surface; allow to dry.

14 Mix the cream, tan, and green glazes following this recipe:
    1 part paint to 3 parts glazing liquid (see "Mixing Glazes,"
    page 16).

15 Using the 3-inch chip brush, apply some of each glaze to
    the surface in a random, natural pattern, brushing directly
    over the wrinkles.

16 Using a slightly wrinkled cheesecloth pom-pom (page 18),
    rub the glaze over the surface.

17 Rearrange the pom-pom to a clean area of the cheese-
    cloth, and continue rubbing to refine the glazes.

18 Continue applying and rubbing the glazes to complete
    the room; allow to dry.

textured imprints

Weathered, yet delicate, this old-world finish is easy to achieve using joint compound, glaze, and artificial leaves. For well-defined imprints, look for leaves with prominent veining and pronounced texture. ◆ You'll need more joint compound than indicated on the container for your square footage because you must apply it thicker than usual. ◆ If your walls are heavily textured, apply a preliminary coat of compound to smooth the surface.

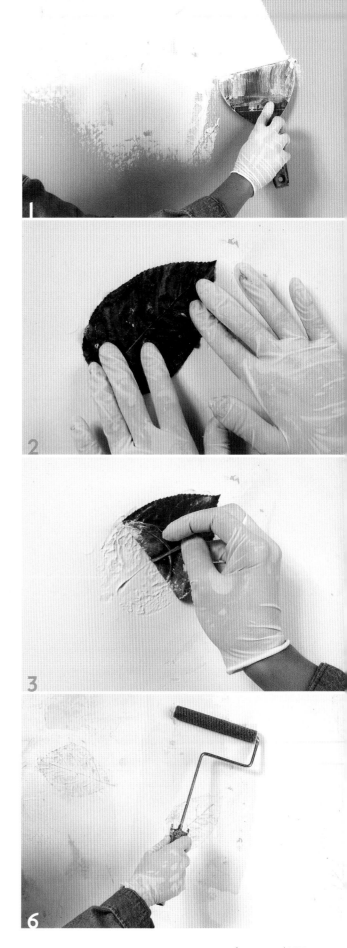

imprinting the leaves

1   Sand the edge and corners of the taping knife. Use the kitchen spatula to transfer some of the joint compound from its container to the plaster trough; close the container. Apply the joint compound to the wall with the taping knife, using a sweeping pattern over an area 3 by 3 feet.

2   Pour water into the shallow dish, and set it in a convenient place. Wet the back of one leaf. Press the leaf into the joint compound, making sure the leaf's veining and texture are embedded. Work out any trapped air with your fingers.

3   Slowly and gently peel the leaf away from the surface, starting with the stem.

4   Press the remaining leaves into the joint compound in a random or organized pattern, depending on the look you want to achieve. Peel away the leaves, starting with the stems. Rinse the leaves in the dish to reuse.

5   Continuing to work in sections, apply the joint compound and press the leaves into the surface to complete the room. The room will become humid as the compound dries, so open windows and doors and set up fans to speed drying and vent the fumes. Allow to dry overnight.

6   Using the mini-roller, apply the shellac over the compound to seal it. Leave the room when finished to avoid the fumes. Allow to dry according to the manufacturer's instructions.

steps continue >

glazing the walls

7 Mix the glaze using the light green and burnt umber universal tints and glazing liquid (see "Mixing Glazes," page 16). Add a little water to the glaze to make it more watercolor-like. You can also make the glaze using 1 part green latex paint, 7 parts glazing liquid, and a little water. The effect will be slightly less transparent than a glaze made with universal tints.

8 Using the 3-inch chip brush, apply the glaze in a loose pattern over the leaf imprints and portions of the open areas.

9 Using a flat cheesecloth pom-pom (page 18), push the glaze back and forth over the surface so the color catches in the imprints.

10 Also push the glaze over the surface in the open areas in a light scrubbing motion.

11 Continue working the surface with the pom-pom to even out the color.

12 Mix a small amount of glazing liquid with a little bronzing powder. Using the round brush, lightly brush the metallic glaze over portions of each leaf to create highlights.

13 Continue applying the metallic glaze to complete the room.

tip ALTHOUGH THE JOINT COMPOUND HAS BEEN SEALED, ITS SLIGHTLY IRREGULAR SURFACE DRAWS THE WATER OUT OF THE CHEESECLOTH, MAKING IT MORE DIFFICULT TO MANIPULATE THE GLAZE. RINSE THE POM-POM OFTEN TO REMOISTEN THE CHEESECLOTH.

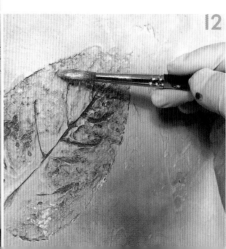

materials

Basic painting supplies
    (page 8)

Chalk in a contrasting color

Kitchen spatula

Wallboard joint compound,
    in smallest quantity

Pastry bag with ¼-inch
    round tip

180-grit sandpaper
    (optional; see Tip,
    page 110)

Standard roller frame with
    9-inch roller cover

Cheesecloth

One 2-inch chip brush

One 4-inch chip brush

Latex primer

Peach latex paint, satin
    finish, for base coat

Coral latex paint, satin
    finish, for top coat

Latex glazing liquid

bas relief

Create this whimsical finish using a pastry bag with a cake-decorating tip as your tool. Don't worry if you're not a pro at decorating cakes—less-than-perfect "frosting" (joint compound) is part of the charm. ◆ *Glaze also comes into play, adding definition to the motifs and a haze of color to the background. This is one technique you should practice directly on your wall to get a feel for how the joint compound adheres to a vertical surface; the wet compound wipes off easily.*

1 Using the standard roller, apply a base coat of peach paint to the walls; allow to dry. Apply a second coat; allow to dry.

2 Draw scrolls and leaves on the walls with the chalk, spacing the motifs as desired.

3 Follow the directions on the package to assemble the pastry bag and tip. Using the kitchen spatula, scoop out enough joint compound to fill the bag approximately two-thirds full; close the container.

4 Holding the bag in both hands, squeeze the compound all the way to the tip. Holding the tip slightly away from the wall, apply the compound along the chalk lines and inside the leaves. Discharge any compound that accumulates at the tip onto a clean rag.

5 Smooth the compound with your index finger. Use a light touch to preserve the shape of the raised lines.

6 Continue to apply the compound to the remaining chalk motifs; allow to dry overnight.

tip FOR A MORE REFINED EFFECT, LIGHTLY SAND THE JOINT COMPOUND WITH 180-GRIT SANDPAPER, OR USE A WET RAG TO SMOOTH OUT IRREGULAR AREAS. (THE MOTIFS SHOWN HERE WERE NOT SANDED OR SMOOTHED.)

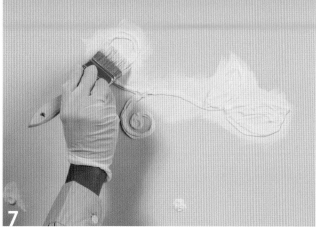

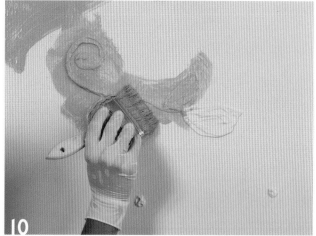

7 Using the 2-inch chip brush, apply a coat of primer to the motifs to seal the joint compound. Feather out the edges of the primer to avoid a halo effect; allow to dry.

8 Using the 2-inch chip brush, apply the peach paint to the primed motifs, feathering out the edges of the paint; allow to dry.

9 Mix the coral glaze following this recipe: I part paint to 3 parts glazing liquid (see "Mixing Glazes," page 16).

10 Using the 4-inch chip brush, apply the glaze to several of the raised motifs and the background. Be sure to brush the glaze well into the nooks and crannies of the joint compound.

11 Using a flat cheesecloth pom-pom, lightly rub the glaze back and forth to work it into the motifs. Without rinsing your pom-pom, rub the background to distribute the glaze across the wall.

12 Repeat on the remaining motifs to complete the walls.

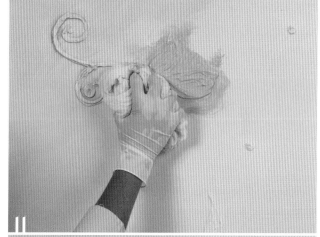

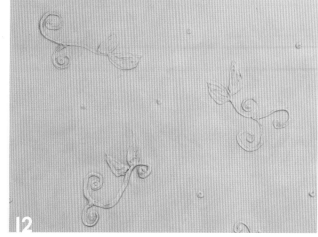

denim

It takes only a few inexpensive paint tools, light and dark blue paint, and glazing liquid to create the look of patchwork denim squares. It starts with measuring, marking, and taping off the squares. A texturing roller takes the place of specialty denim tools; overlapping the paint slightly where the squares meet suggests real seams. ◆ *Because the effect is so striking, you'll probably want to limit it to one wall, as was done in this attic playroom. If you like, add upholsterer's tacks to the corners where the squares meet, to suggest the rivets in blue jeans.*

materials

Basic painting supplies (page 8)

Standard roller frame with 9-inch roller cover

Small roller frame with 4-inch roller cover

One 9-inch texturing roller cover

One 2-inch tapered synthetic paintbrush

Steel tape measure

Plumb bob

Carpenter's level

Pencil

Blue painter's tape, 1 inch wide

Light blue latex paint, satin finish, for base coat

Denim blue latex paint, satin finish, for glaze

Latex glazing liquid

preparing and marking the wall

1 Using the standard roller, apply a base coat of light blue paint to the walls; allow to dry. Apply a second coat; allow to dry.

2 Find the horizontal midpoint of the wall and, with a helper, drop a plumb bob from the ceiling at that point. Mark the center line on the wall with a pencil.

3 Determine the square size. If your wall has a window, use the measurement from the bottom of the windowsill to the top of the baseboard for the square size so you'll have a row of complete squares from the window to the baseboard. If your wall has no window, choose a square size that divides evenly into your ceiling height. Using the steel tape, measure and mark off the squares, starting from the center line.

4 Using the carpenter's level, draw the vertical and horizontal lines for the squares.

5 Tape off every other square, placing the tape on the *outside* of the pencil lines and pressing it firmly against the lines. You will paint these squares first. Put small pieces of tape in the alternate squares to avoid painting them by mistake.

painting the wall

6 Mix 1 part denim blue paint and 1 part glazing liquid (see "Mixing Glazes," page 16). Using the small roller, apply the denim blue glaze to the taped-off squares.

steps continue >

tip TEXTURING ROLLER COVERS HAVE LITTLE LOOPS ON THE SURFACE THAT PRODUCE A DEFINITE DIRECTIONAL PATTERN, OR NAP. EXPERIMENT WITH A TEXTURING ROLLER COVER AND PAINT ON A SAMPLE BOARD (PAGE 19) TO DECIDE WHICH WAY TO SNAP THE COVER ONTO THE ROLLER.

7   Using the standard roller with texturing roller cover, go over the glaze vertically to create the look of denim. Roll in one direction only—either up or down.

8   When the glaze is dry to the touch, remove all the tape. On the light blue squares, apply the denim blue glaze with the small roller.

9   Where the squares meet, slightly overlap the edges of the just-painted squares to create the illusion of seams.

10 Using the standard roller with texturing roller cover, go over the glaze horizontally, rolling in one direction only.

11 At the wall edges and the ceiling line, apply the denim blue glaze with a 2-inch tapered brush. Use a paint key or nail to mimic the effect of the texturing roller cover, moving it in the same direction as the glaze grain, horizontally or verti-cally, depending on which square you're in; allow to dry.

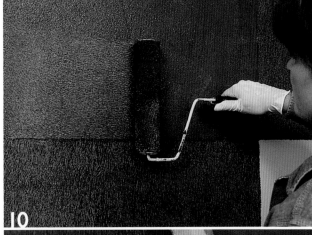

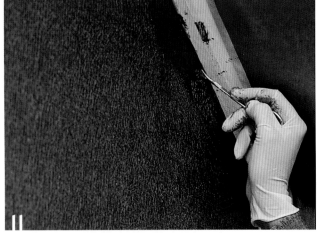

taffeta

A wood-graining "rocker" tool turns a coat of glaze into faux taffeta. The greater the contrast between the base coat (pale pink in this example) and the glaze (medium pink), the more pronounced the visual texture. ◆ You'll need to practice with the tool to get a feel for it; the package will include instructions. Taping off the wall and working in alternate sections helps to keep the pattern straight up and down. Choose a section width that divides evenly into the width of the wall, such as 20-inch sections on a 10-foot-wide wall.

1. Using the standard roller, apply a base coat of pale pink paint to the walls; allow to dry. Apply a second coat; allow to dry.

2. Using the carpenter's level, acrylic rotary ruler, and pencil, measure and lightly mark the section widths across the wall. Tape off alternate sections, as shown below.

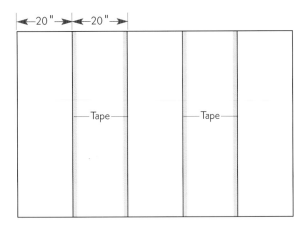

←20″→ ←20″→

—Tape— —Tape—

3. Mix the glaze following this recipe: I part paint, 3 parts glazing liquid, and a little water (see "Mixing Glazes," page 16).

4. Begin in a corner, at the upper edge of the wall. Using the 4-inch chip brush, cut in with the glaze at the corner, ceiling line, and baseboard of the first section.

5. Using the mini-roller and working in the first section, roll the glaze down the length of the wall in straight, even passes. On the final pass, roll just over the edge of the first piece of tape.

5

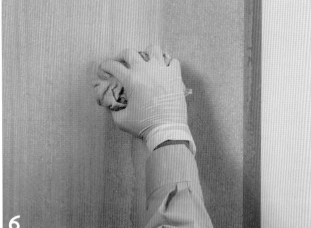

6

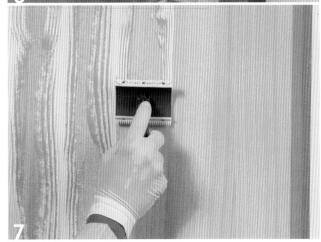

7

6. With a damp, flat cheesecloth pom-pom, drag the glaze down the length of the wall.

7. Using the wood-graining tool, drag the glaze the length of the wall, rocking the tool back and forth to create a pattern.

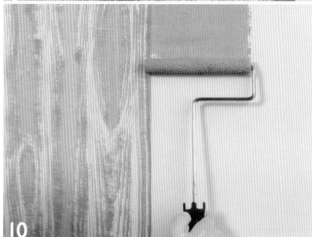

8 Holding the blender brush slightly to the side, vigorously sweep across the surface horizontally to soften and blend the glaze.

tip AT THIS POINT THE GLAZE IS VERY THIN, SO WORK QUICKLY WITH THE BLENDER BRUSH BEFORE THE GLAZE DRIES.

9 Continue to roll and drag the remaining taped-off sections; allow to dry to the touch. Remove the tape.

10 Repeat the process in the first unglazed section, rolling barely over the edges of the completed section on either side.

11 Drag the glaze with the cheesecloth pom-pom, followed by the wood-graining tool. Continue to roll and drag the remaining sections.

12 Repeat the process on the remaining walls to complete the room.

materials

Basic painting supplies
    (page 8)

Stencil plastic

Pencil

One 6- by 24-inch acrylic
    rotary ruler and cutting
    mat (page 9)

Craft knife

Pale colored pencil

Blue painter's tape,
    1 inch wide

Mini-roller frame with
    6-inch roller cover, or
    2½-inch paintbrush

White latex paint, matte
    or eggshell finish, for
    background

Four coordinated stamps
    (see Resources,
    page 144)

Four colored stamp pads

Yellow-green acrylic paint

Small artist's brush

wildflower stamps

Stamping is a quick-and-easy technique for decorating walls in a small room. Stores devoted to stamp and paper crafts offer an astonishing selection of stamps and stamp-pad colors. ◆ *Real pressed flowers inspired the wildflower stamps shown here; the irregular background was made using a "window" stencil, torn painter's tape, and white paint. One important note: Smooth walls are a must for successful stamping.*

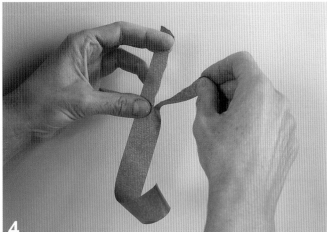

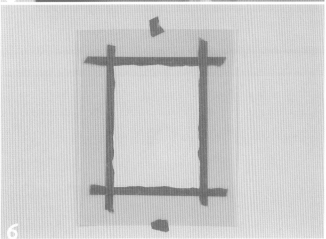

1   Based on the size of your stamps, determine the size of the window opening. The stamps shown here measure 4 by 4 inches when grouped; the window opening measures 5½ by 7½ inches, with several inches of stencil "frame" around the opening.

2   Using the pencil, rotary equipment, and craft knife, measure, mark, and cut the window stencil.

3   Anchor the stencil to the wall with pieces of blue painter's tape.

4   Tear a piece of blue painter's tape in half lengthwise, creating a ragged edge.

5   With the ragged edge just over the lower edge of the window opening, adhere the tape to the wall. Run your fingers over the ragged edge to make sure it is firmly adhered.

6   Repeat with torn tape on the remaining edges of the opening.

7   Using the base-coat color of the wall (lavender in this example), paint the ragged edges of the tape to prevent the white paint from seeping under in the next step (see "A Tape Trick," page 15).

steps continue >

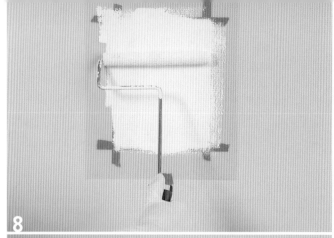

8 Using the mini-roller or 2½-inch paintbrush, apply the white paint to the wall, through the opening; allow to dry. Apply a second coat, if necessary; allow to dry.

9 Carefully remove the stencil and tape to reveal the white background for the stamps.

10 From the leftover stencil plastic, cut a square equal to the size of the stamps grouped. Position the square in the background as desired and lightly draw around the edges with the colored pencil.

11 Press the first stamp firmly into one of the stamp pads several times to load the surface with ink. Position the stamp over the background, using the drawn lines as a guide.

tip THE MOST COMMON BEGINNER MISTAKE IS TO FAIL TO PRESS THE STAMP INTO THE PAD FIRMLY ENOUGH.

12 Press the stamp firmly against the wall; lift the stamp.

13 Repeat with the remaining stamps.

14 Using the small artist's brush, paint the marked lines with the yellow-green acrylic paint.

allover stencil

You'll find a wealth of large-scale, repeat stencil designs online; the stencil shown here measures 26 by 26 inches. Placement planning is essential, so be sure to read the Tip on page 122 before you begin. ◆ *This wall has a one-color glaze as the base coat, but it's simpler to apply two coats of latex paint. Acrylic metallic paint for the gold glaze dries quickly, allowing you to remove and reposition the stencil without waiting.*

materials

- Basic painting supplies (page 8)
- Standard roller frame with 9-inch roller cover
- Repositionable spray adhesive
- Stencil (see Resources, page 144)
- Carpenter's level
- One 4-inch chip brush
- One 2-inch chip brush
- Cheesecloth
- Light tan latex paint, satin finish, for base coat
- Gold metallic acrylic paint for stencil glaze
- Universal tints in black and burnt sienna (dark brown) for stencil glaze
- Dark taupe latex paint, satin finish, for overglaze
- Latex glazing liquid

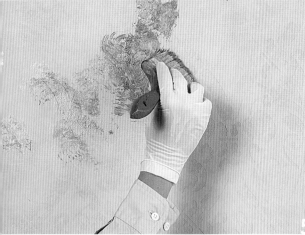

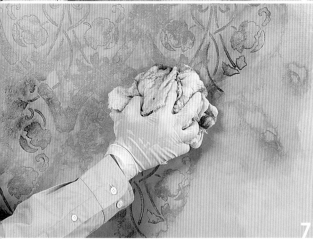

technique

1   Using the standard roller, apply a base coat of light tan paint to the walls; allow to dry. Apply a second coat; allow to dry.

tip IF YOU BEGIN STENCILING IN ONE CORNER AND WORK YOUR WAY AROUND THE ROOM, THE EDGES OF THE DESIGN ARE UNLIKELY TO MATCH WHEN YOU REACH YOUR STARTING POINT. FOR THAT REASON, BEGIN IN AN INCONSPICUOUS SPOT, SUCH AS OVER A DOOR.

2   Study your stencil to find the registration marks or alignment motifs. Spray the back of the stencil with repositionable spray adhesive, following the manufacturer's directions.

3   Using the carpenter's level, position the stencil on the wall; smooth the stencil firmly with your hands to adhere it. Using a clean folded cloth, smooth the stencil again.

4   Mix the gold metallic glaze using 1 part gold metallic paint and 1 part glazing liquid. Mix the black-brown glaze using the black and burnt sienna universal tints and glazing liquid (see "Mixing Glazes," page 16).

5   Using the 4-inch chip brush in a quick tapping motion, stipple the gold metallic glaze onto the wall, through the stencil. Strive for a mottled, slightly irregular look rather than uniform color.

6   Stipple the black-brown glaze through the stencil using the 2-inch chip brush to create dark accents.

7   Using a wrinkled cheesecloth pom-pom (page 18), lightly rub the glazes to erase some of the color.

tip USE THE LEVEL EACH TIME YOU REPOSITION THE STENCIL TO MAKE SURE THE PATTERN ISN'T GOING UPHILL OR DOWNHILL. FUDGE THE PLACEMENT OF THE STENCIL IF NEEDED TO COMPENSATE; SLIGHT IRREGULARITIES WILL NOT BE NOTICEABLE.

8 Remove the stencil. The completed section will look similar to the one shown here, with irregular edges where the pattern repeats.

9 Carefully align the stencil according to the pattern repeat and registration marks or motifs; adhere the stencil to the wall.

10 Repeat the stippling and rubbing steps with the gold and black-brown glazes; remove the stencil.

11 Continue working in the same manner, reapplying the adhesive as needed, to complete the walls; allow to dry.

12 Mix the overglaze using I part paint to 2 parts glazing liquid.

13 Using the 4-inch chip brush, apply the glaze randomly over an area approximately 2 by 2 feet. Leave some areas open to create a slightly mottled effect.

14 Using a flat cheesecloth pom-pom, pounce and lightly rub the glaze over the surface. Feather and blend the glaze at the edges.

15 Continue working in the same manner, section by section, to complete the walls.

petroglyph walls

Abstract motifs add a splash of color to neutral walls and bring to mind primitive rock drawings. Enlarge the shapes shown here using the patterns provided on the following pages or draw your own. If you opt to create original designs, keep them simple and chunky for maximum impact. Latex paint has a tendency to seep under stencils, so plan to touch up the edges of the motifs with your wall paint and a small paintbrush.

1   Enlarge the patterns on pages 126–127 to the indicated dimensions at a photocopy shop. Lay stencil plastic over each motif, and trace the lines with the felt-tip marker.

2   Working on the rotary cutting mat, cut along the lines with the craft knife.

3   Cover your work surface with paper towels. Spray the back of a stencil with repositionable adhesive.

4   Position the stencil on the wall and press firmly to adhere. Dip the stencil brush into the paint, and then dab the brush on paper towels to remove the excess.

5   Holding the stencil brush perpendicular to the wall, pounce (dab) the paint onto the wall through the cutout area of the stencil. Be careful not to push the paint under the edges of the stencil.

6   Remove the stencil and allow the paint to dry.

7   Repeat Steps 3–6 to stencil the other motifs on the wall. Touch up the edges, if needed, with your wall paint.

project continues >

$2\frac{3}{8}''$

$15\frac{1}{4}''$

$11\frac{3}{4}''$

Stencil patterns.
See Step 1 on page 125.

11"

tip VARY THE HEIGHT AND SPACING OF THE MOTIFS FOR A RANDOM EFFECT. (MAP OUT THE PLACEMENT AHEAD OF TIME IF YOU LACK THE CONFIDENCE TO STENCIL AS YOU GO.) ALSO VARY THE ANGLE OF THE MOTIFS TO GIVE THE WALLS VITALITY AND AN ELEMENT OF SURPRISE.

10"

12¼"

materials

Basic painting supplies
(page 8)

Standard roller frame with
9-inch roller cover

Peach latex paint, satin
finish, for base coat

Stencil (see Resources,
page 144)

Repositionable spray
adhesive

Concentrated liquid acrylic
paints* in desired colors

Latex glazing liquid
(optional; see Step 4)

Small containers for paint

Small, medium, and large
stencil brushes

* Buy the smallest sizes available; it
takes very little paint to stencil.

floating stencil
A stencil with "floating" motifs adds bursts of color and pattern to any room. You'll find a wide array of stencils in craft stores and on the Internet. Concentrated liquid acrylic paints for artists have the brightest color; acrylic craft paints tend to be more subdued. ◆ *It's essential that you adhere the stencil, especially the narrow pieces, firmly to the surface to prevent the paint from seeping under it. If your walls are textured, be sure to test the stencil in an inconspicuous area before you begin.*

1 Using the standard roller, apply a base coat of peach paint to the walls; allow to dry. Apply a second coat; allow to dry.

2 Spray the back of the stencil with the repositionable spray adhesive, following the manufacturer's directions.

3 Position the stencil and press it firmly against the wall; anchor the corners with painter's tape. Using moderate pressure, carefully run your finger over the edges of the design to adhere them to the surface. Be sure all edges are adhered before you proceed.

4 Start with the largest shape and the large stencil brush. Transfer a very small amount of the first paint to a small container; add a few drops of glaze, if desired, to lighten the color. Swirl the tips of the brush in the paint; then swirl the brush onto a folded paper towel to disperse the paint.

5 Begin with the brush perpendicular to the surface of the stencil plastic, just beyond the edges of the motif. Working into the motif, swirl the paint through the stencil. Pounce the surface to even out the colors.

6 Continue working in the same manner with the remaining paints, using the medium and small brushes for the smaller shapes.

7 Peel the stencil from the wall; reposition it and continue painting to complete the wall.

lime paint

Paint that contains lime behaves differently from other paints. When wet, it appears dark and dull; as it dries, it blooms, creating a lighter, slightly mottled effect. The color continues to evolve until the walls are sealed. The raised motifs are made using stencils and joint compound; for a uniform surface, smooth the walls first with a layer of compound.

materials

Basic painting supplies (page 8)

Stencil plastic for each pattern

Permanent marker

Rotary cutting mat (page 9)

Craft knife

Repositionable spray adhesive

Pushpins

One 4-inch taping knife

Wallboard joint compound

Sanding block, medium-fine grit

Undercoat sealer*

Standard roller frame with 9-inch roller cover

One 2½-inch synthetic paintbrush

Lime paint (see Resources, page 144)

One 6-inch box brush

Clear acrylic sealer, matte finish *

*Use sealers recommended by the lime paint manufacturer.

making the patterns

1 Enlarge the patterns on pages 133–135 to the indicated dimensions at a photocopy shop.

2 Determine the placement of the motifs and lightly mark the walls. Strive for varied angles and random distribution of shapes.

making the stencils

3 Lay stencil plastic over the enlarged pattern, allowing several inches of plastic beyond the pattern's rectangular outline. Trace the leaf and the rectangle with the permanent marker.

4 Working on the rotary cutting mat, cut on the lines using the craft knife. Keep the leaf shape and the outer "frame" piece. (You can see these two pieces in photo 6.) Set aside the piece in between.

applying the compound

5 Cover your work surface with paper towels. Spray the back of each part of the stencil with repositionable adhesive.

6 Position the leaf and the outer piece and press firmly to adhere. Insert a pushpin at one end of the leaf to allow you to pull it away once it's covered with joint compound.

7 Using the taping knife, apply the compound to the wall, over the stencil plastic and through the open area. Spread the compound $\frac{1}{16}$ to $\frac{1}{8}$ inch thick, striving for a slightly irregular surface, as if frosting a cake. Go over the area several times to release any air bubbles.

8 Carefully lift the frame piece. Gently pull out the pushpin and lift the leaf, revealing the recessed motif.

9 Your recessed motif should look like the one shown here.

steps continue >

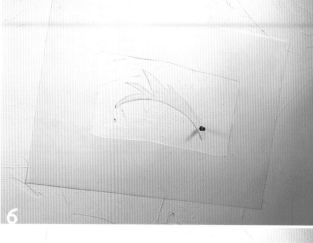

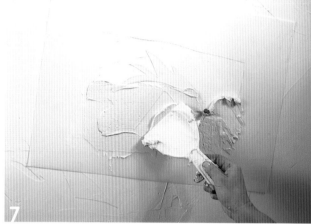

10. Wash the compound off the stencil pieces and wipe them dry.

11. Stencil the remaining motifs in the same way. Allow the compound to dry overnight, until it is light and uniform in color.

12. Using the sanding block, lightly sand the edges of each motif and any other areas that are noticeably rough.

painting the walls

13. Apply the undercoat sealer with the paint roller according to the manufacturer's instructions. Work the sealer into the recessed areas with the 2½-inch paintbrush; allow to dry.

tip TO MAINTAIN A WET EDGE AND PREVENT STOP-AND-START LINES WHEN PAINTING, HAVE A HELPER APPLY THE LIME PAINT AT THE CEILING LINE AND IN THE CORNERS WITH THE 2½-INCH BRUSH WHILE YOU COVER THE LARGE AREAS WITH THE BOX BRUSH.

14. Apply the lime paint with the 6-inch box brush in a broad, crosshatching motion. Be sure to work the paint into the recessed areas. Allow to dry for 6 hours. Apply a second and a third coat, allowing at least 6 hours between coats.

15. Using the paint roller or box brush, apply the matte sealer. (Avoid overloading the roller or the brush with sealer—it tends to run.) Use the 2½-inch brush to work the sealer into the recessed areas. Don't be alarmed at the color of the sealer; it goes on milky (and darkens the paint), but it all dries to the proper color.

12¼"

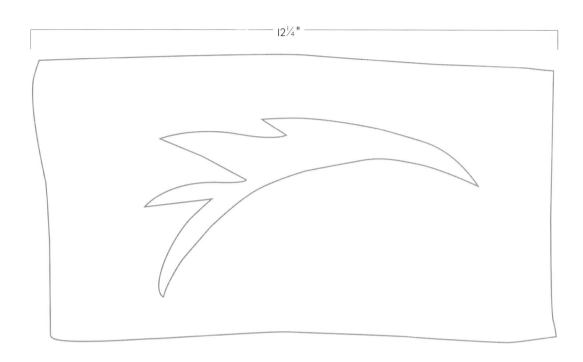

13⅛"

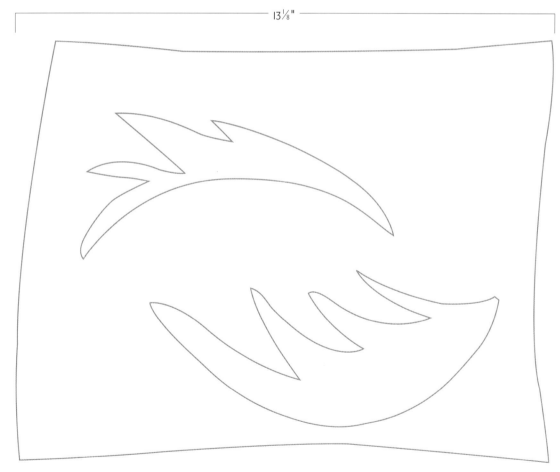

Stencil patterns. See Step 1 on page 131. (The rectangles above can also be combined
with the larger motifs on the following pages; see photo on page 130.)

project continues >

$11\frac{3}{8}"$

$11\frac{3}{8}"$

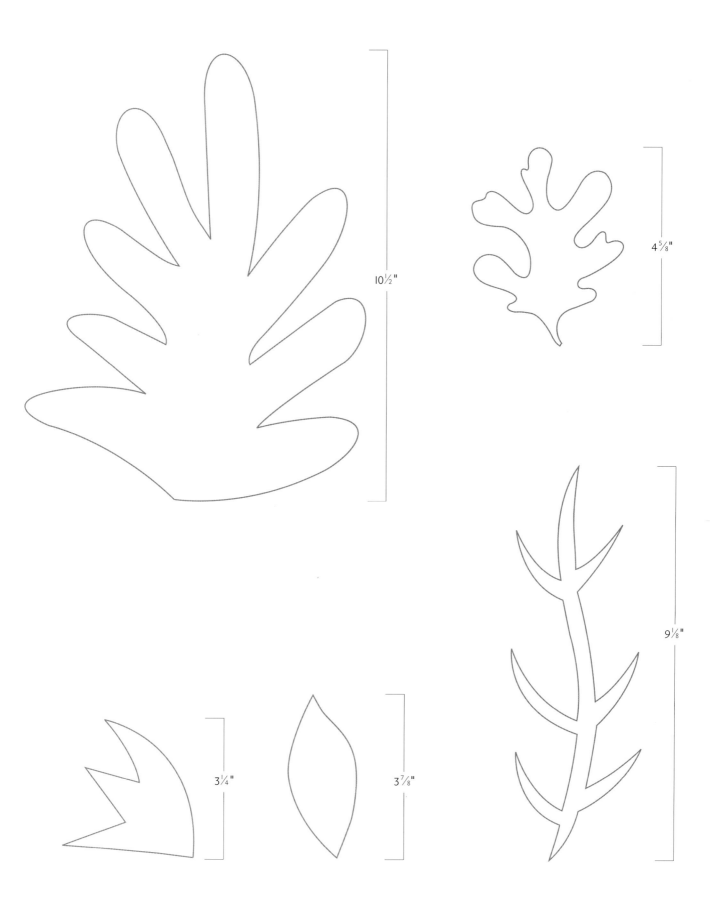

10½"

4⅝"

9⅛"

3¼"

3⅞"

materials

Basic painting supplies
(page 8)

Steel tape measure

Carpenter's level

Long straightedge*

Pencil

Standard roller frame with
9-inch roller cover

Mini-roller frame with
6-inch roller cover

Blue painter's tape,
1 inch wide

White latex paint,
eggshell or pearl finish,
for base coat

Yellow, peach, pink, mauve,
violet, aqua, and lime
green latex paint, satin
finish, for color blocks

Gum eraser

*A 6-foot metal straightedge is ideal.

color blocks
This painterly treatment requires neither precision nor artistic ability. Blue painter's tape provides a visual guide for rolling on the loose squares of color. ◆ For a harmonious effect, choose colors at the same location on each paint strip, such as the third color from the top. This technique is best on a windowless, focal-point wall, with the remaining walls painted a solid color. Be sure to practice on a sample board (page 19) before you begin.

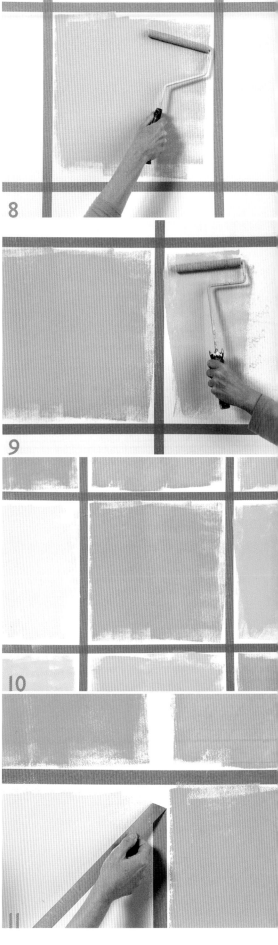

1. Using the standard roller, apply a base coat of white paint to the walls; allow to dry. Apply a second coat; allow to dry.

2. Measure the wall and determine a square size that divides evenly into the width and height of the wall. (You will not detect the difference if the shapes are not truly square.)

3. Using the carpenter's level, long straightedge, and pencil, measure and very lightly mark the squares on the wall.

4. Apply the 1-inch blue painter's tape over the lines, not along the edges. It's not necessary to be precise; the tape is only a guide.

5. Make a sketch of your wall and the number of squares. Decide where to place the colors, and mark them on the sketch. Make sure the colors will be evenly distributed across the wall.

6. Pour a small amount of the first color into the paint tray; roll the mini-roller in the paint, being careful not to overload it.

7. Practice on the sample board to determine how much paint you'll need on the roller to achieve the look you like. The squares shown here have a "dry roller" look on some of the edges, the result of using a minimum of paint.

8. Paint the first square on the wall, rolling close to—but not over— the painter's tape. Strive for a loose effect, with some of the white base coat showing through. (Resist the urge to go over the square again and again or you will lose the casual look.) Paint the remaining squares marked for this color.

9. Paint the squares marked for the second color in the same manner.

10. Paint the remaining squares using the other colors; allow to dry.

11. Remove the tape.

12. Carefully erase the marked lines with the gum eraser.

color blending

A sheepskin decorative painting tool blends two colors of paint in one step for a quick-and-easy finish. It's not necessary to apply a base coat to your walls; the paint covers the existing wall color. ◆ If you choose two colors from the same paint strip, make sure they are separated by three or more colors for adequate contrast.

materials

Basic painting supplies, minus the paint tray, plus an additional bucket (page 8)

The Woolie™ paint tool (see "Resources," page 144)

Light periwinkle latex paint, satin finish

Medium-dark periwinkle latex paint, satin finish

One 6-inch synthetic paintbrush

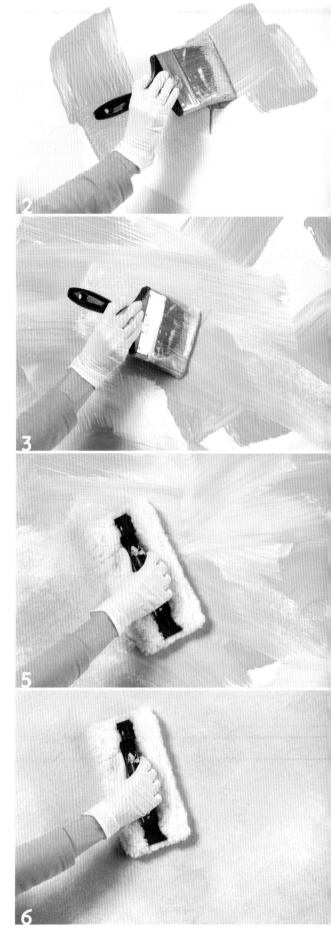

1   Transfer each paint to a bucket. Add 1½ cups of water to each gallon of paint; stir to mix thoroughly.

2   Using the 6-inch brush, apply the light periwinkle paint thickly in short, random strokes over an area 4 by 4 feet, leaving some of the existing color showing. Repeat the process by applying the medium-dark periwinkle paint over some of the light paint and the remaining open areas. Don't be concerned about paint drips; they will be incorporated as you blend the colors.

3   Blend the paint slightly with the brush in wide, sweeping strokes; do not overblend.

4   Brush a little of each paint onto the Woolie™ paint tool, including the sides, to moisten the sheepskin.

5   Using the tool in a quick tapping motion, pounce the surface to blend the paint colors slightly. Use the edge of the tool to apply paint at the ceiling line and baseboards and into the corners. If you want a finish with strong visual texture, stop at this point.

6   Continue pouncing the surface to refine the visual texture, being careful not to overblend the colors.

tip IF YOU ACCIDENTALLY OVERBLEND, ADD A BIT OF THE LIGHT OR THE MEDIUM-DARK PAINT AND POUNCE LIGHTLY TO CREATE HIGHS (AREAS OF LIGHTER COLOR) AND LOWS (AREAS OF DARKER COLOR).

7   Continue working in the same manner to complete the walls; allow to dry.

rickrack stencil

Yellow and aqua stripes provide a pretty backdrop for a jumbo rickrack stencil. The stripes measure 4½ and 7½ inches wide; the stencil is also 4½ inches wide, making it easy to line up the edges of the stencil with the edges of the stripes. ◆ *The step-by-step photos show how to change colors within one rickrack stripe, but you can stencil each stripe using just one color, as shown below.*

materials

Basic painting supplies
   (page 8)

Standard roller frame with
   9-inch roller cover

Carpenter's level

One 6 by 24-inch acrylic
   rotary ruler (page 9)

3- or 6-foot straightedge

Pencil

Blue painter's tape,
   1 inch wide

Putty knife

Mini-roller frame with
   6-inch roller cover

One 1-inch chip brush

Yellow latex paint, satin
   finish, for base coat

Aqua latex paint, satin
   finish, for stripes

Stencil plastic, at least
   6 by 20 inches

Permanent marker

Small, sharp scissors

Repositionable spray
   adhesive

One 6- by 6-inch acrylic
   rotary ruler (page 9)

Stencil creams

Paper towels

One 1-inch stencil brush

One ¼-inch stencil brush

1 Using the standard roller, apply a base coat of yellow paint to the walls; allow
   to dry. Apply a second coat; allow to dry.

2 Refer to "A Tape Trick," page 15, as you work through the following steps. Using
   the carpenter's level, long straightedge, and pencil, measure and lightly mark the
   stripes on the wall.

3 To tape off the 7½-inch aqua stripes, position the edges of the tape on the marked
   lines, with the tape itself in the yellow areas. Using the putty knife, burnish the
   edges to be painted.

4 Using the yellow paint and the chip brush, paint the edges of the tape to prevent
   the aqua paint from seeping under in the next step.

5 Using the mini-roller, paint the aqua stripes; allow to dry. Apply a second coat;
   allow to dry. Remove the tape.

6 Trace two copies of the rickrack pattern, and tape the pieces together to make
   one long pattern. Lay the stencil plastic over the pattern, and trace the lines using
   the permanent marker. Using the scissors, carefully cut out the right and left sides
   of the rickrack stencil on the lines. Label the sides.

7 Spray the wrong sides of the stencils with the repositionable spray adhesive,
   following the manufacturer's directions.

8 Begin at the ceiling line. (For clarity, the following photos show the wall farther
   down.) Place the edge of the left stencil on the edge of the first yellow stripe.
   Anchor with a piece of painter's tape; press to adhere the stencil to the wall.

steps continue >

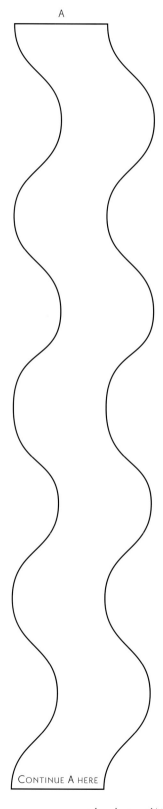

A

CONTINUE A HERE

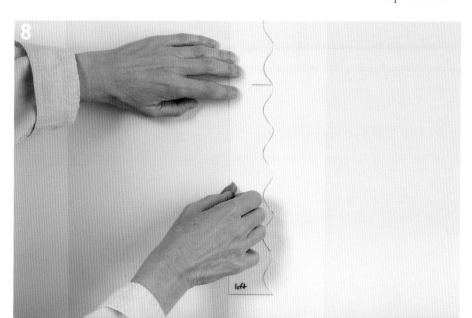

rickrack stencil 141

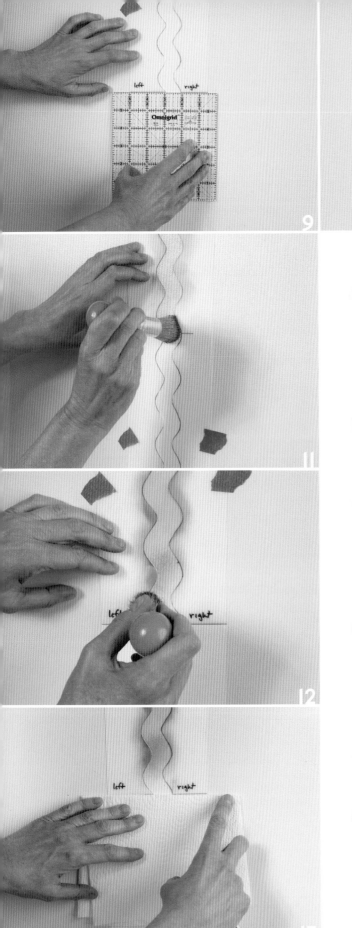

9 Align the rotary ruler with the end of the left stencil as shown; also align the markings on the ruler with both edges of the yellow stripe, making the ruler level. Place the edge of the right stencil on the right edge of the yellow stripe, as shown, with the end aligned with the ruler. Anchor and adhere the stencil to the wall.

10 Swirl the bristles of the 1-inch stencil brush in the stencil cream. Swirl the brush onto a folded paper towel to disperse the cream.

11 Begin with the brush perpendicular to the surface of the stencil plastic, just over the cut edge. Working into the design, swirl the cream through the stencil.

12 To change colors, wash and dry the brush. Begin the new color where the previous color ends; continue stenciling.

13 When you reach the end of the stencil, place a folded paper towel as shown to protect the wall area below. Finish applying the cream. Remove the stencils

14 Reposition the stencils to continue the design; adhere to the wall.

15 To prevent the cream from going outside the design, use the ¼-inch stencil brush to begin stenciling again.

16 Continue down the yellow stripe in the same manner. As you approach the baseboard, bend the stencil to keep it flat against the wall. Repeat the process to stencil the remaining stripes.

train mural

Painting an original mural takes talent and time, but you can create the same graphic effect using a mural kit (see "Resources," page 144). The kit provides instructions, color guide, full-size pattern, alignment tape, tracing pencil, tapered paintbrush, and black marker. You will need to purchase acrylic craft paint.

see "Resources," page 144

technique

1 Following the instructions in the kit, carefully position the pattern on the wall; adhere with the tape.

2 Transfer the design to the wall by tracing the lines using the tracing pencil.

3 Following the color guide, paint the wall using acrylic craft paint and the tapered paintbrush.

4 Once the paint is dry, outline the design with the black marker.

index

take note

RESOURCES

Page 118: Wildflower stamps

Hero Arts
800-822-4376
www.heroarts.com

Page 119: Entwined trellis stencil

Royal Design Studio
800-747-9767
www.royaldesignstudio.com

page 126: Daisy stencil

The Stencil Library
www.stencil-library.com

page 128: Lime paint and sealers

Portola Paints & Glazes
818-623-9053
www.portolapaints.com

page 136: Sheepskin painting tool

The Woolie
888-596-6543
www.woolie.com

page 143: Mural kits

HDA, Inc.
877-925-5687
www.muralsbywallart.com